To
Marie,
Bob, Greg and Shawna
who have made my life
one very big special event.

And to
DUCT® TAPE
Thanks for sticking by us
and for holding so many
events together
(. . . as well as for giving me a great book cover!)

TABLE OF CONTENTS
Your Event Fitness Program

Four Wishes • There's a Place for Us • Owning Up • Negative to Positive Poles • Positioning Pronouns in the Responsible Case • Reading the Same Language • What's the Difference? • Wherefore Art Thou? • By the Books • What Are You Going to Read About? • Fitness as a Theme • Here's Your Exam Chart •

And Now for the Real Workout • You WILL Have Fun! • It's Time for the RFP • Making Your RFP Information Fit • RFP Starting Points • RFP Components for All Projects • REQUEST FOR PROPOSAL RESPONSE OUTLINE • And Now Take Your Pick from My RFPs • EVENT PROJECTS:

1. FESTIVAL UNDER FIRE
2. STARS, STRIPES AND FUN FOREVER
3. GAMES PEOPLE WILL PLAY
4. EVENT MAKE-OVER
5. PLANNING RELIGIOUSLY
6. GOLF FOR A CHANGE
7. BOUQUETS TO THE WINNERS
8. WORDS ABOUT A FESTIVAL ABOUT WORDS
9. LOST AND FOUND HOURS CELEBRATION
10. NATIONAL CONDOM WEEK
11. EARTH DAY
12. THE GREAT AMERICAN MONEY FESTIVAL
13. A PRINCELY AND PRINCESSLY AFFAIR
14. NEW-PRODUCT SERIAL EVENT
15. YOU'RE KIDDING YOURSELF
16. MUSIC TO EVERYBODY'S EARS

Alternative: Reality Checks as Wake-Up Calls •

Sample Media Release
Sample Media Advisory

CHAPTER 5: AEROBICS FOR EVENT HEARTS

For Enforced Absentees • On-Site, For Special Guests • Sunday Mornings • Cautions on Cause Marketing • Having a Good Neighbor's Heart • Merchants of Menace: Invitations to Terror • A Plan for All Seasons • High Priority: Make Nature Second Nature

CHAPTER 6: IMPROVING ORGANIZATIONAL SET-UPS

Organizational Flab? Or Too Lean and Mean? • Attempting Reorganization • S-L-O-W Expectations • Working Out "Turfism" Spasms • Meet Ms. Ruthless and Mr. Monster • You May Have to Use the Snake • "Virulent Ownership" • Battling Battle-Bound Boards • Why Micro is so Macro • The Political Godfather • So What's New? Nothing! •

Finding and Managing Volunteers

Recruiting Executive Volunteers • Mining for Volunteers • Volunteer Perks • Managing Volunteers • Shifts, To the Right Decision • Let's Talk Training • An Executive Council? Consider it • Notes on Following Committee Descriptions

Sample Committee Descriptions

1. Executive Director / Executive Volunteer
2. Quality Protection
3. Marketing
4. Sponsorship
5. Site Preparation
6. Maintenance
7. Finance
8. Vendors
9. Human Resources
10. Supplies
11. Transportation
12. Communications
13. Security and Safety
14. Entertainment
15. Group Attendance
16. Hospitality
17. Event Extension
18. Sports
19. Awards and Prizes

CHAPTER 7: ENDING UP ON THE TREADMILL

1. LENGTH OF EVENTS
2. SINGLE- VS. MULTIPLE-EVENT SITES
3. IDEAL SITE COMPONENTS
4. SCRAPS OVER SCRIPT
5. BUDGETS FROM THE OUTSIDE IN
6. AN OPEN LETTER TO SPONSORS
7. LOATHSOME *LOP*SIDEDNESS
8. WIN OR LOSE WITH BOOZE?
9. IT'S YOUR CALL
10. DETAILS, DETAILS, DETAILS
11. UNWANTED: SPECIAL EVENTS
2. THERE ARE TOO MANY EVENTS RIGHT NOW
13. MERGERS
14. CAN AN EVENT BECOME TOO LARGE?
15. RAIN TIMES TWO
16. EVENT PACING

FIT TO BE TRIED

FOUR WISHES

To whomever is handing them out these days, I'm asking for four wishes to be granted — in your best interests and mine. (Once upon a time three was the norm. No longer. Greed or inflation . . . maybe both.) They are:

- That *SPECIAL EVENTS: Making Them Fit in the 21st Century* will serve existing events with a rehab blueprint, designed to pump new vitality and vigor—*through quality*—into those standing events;

- That this book will also help events still in prenatal stages to start off as healthy, wholesome youngsters, living long and quality-filled lives that were begun or revitalized on the cusp of the new millennium;

- Very important, that it will provide students of special events with a solid basis on which to start careers in this exciting, fast-growing, highly rewarding and challenging field;

- And finally, that all of us will have lots of fun as we work our way together through this book. Events are not serious business unless they're fun for everyone, even while they're being critically analyzed.

THERE'S A PLACE FOR US

Special events and family-style amusement/theme parks are, by and large, today's last bastions of true-to-the-meaning *family entertainment*.[1] Fortunately, with few exceptions, they are gloriously color*less* . . . no blue language, no red-faced frowns, no white-knuckles bracing for the next nude scene, no blood-splashed sets, no flesh-colored bed action, no purple violence, no green hatred.

Special events and family parks provide the *most personal* of all entertainment vehicles. No others quite match their abilities to put "entertained" people face-to-face with each other, with their entertainers (frequently interactively) and with people running the shows.

There are several hundred amusement/theme parks in this country. Depending on how you count them, there are upwards of *15,000 special events.* It's most important to remember this: events virtually always "play on their home court," which definitely gives them a prime advantage over all other entertainment formats. Parks range from pretty costly to outrageously expensive, whereas nearly all special events are free, thanks to the generosity of sponsors. If they're not, then they post relatively low admission prices.

A genius who greatly impacted the whole world of entertainment (and my own personal and professional life) was the late Walt Disney, the consummate entertainer, the ultimate creative eventer, the greatest "Understander of People." Walt often noted that he hadn't invented the amusement park, but the world agrees that he *did* revolutionize it with Disneyland's opening in 1955. Entertainment hasn't been the same since.

He introduced uncompromising quality, squeaky cleanliness, certain safety, and the best of all-age, really entertaining entertainment. Further, Disney "theming" became an event criterion, a subject I'll present for depth consideration later on.

It's not very likely that special events can be improved through the efforts of just one person. There's not much of a chance that there will ever be a Walt Disney counterpart for this industry. Reasons: there are too many varieties of events, too many in number within each variety, they're too spread out, too segmented— a thousand variations on the event theme and its components. There is not an industry headquarters from which a Disney-type can require measures of improvement. With few exceptions, special events are independent, non-chain operations. Which may be one of their strongest strengths.

That means that there's a monumentally important place for us, you and me . . . a real opportunity. We can collectively keep on improving our own events and helping others do so with theirs. We can make them the most accessible, affordable, high-quality, *family-specific* entertainment opportunities on earth — a source of community pride and slit-eyed envy by others in the field. Very often envy engenders excellence.

It is the objective of promoting the steady improvement of event quality that is this book's reason for being. Like a bee, I hope to use it to pollinate event flowers by taking ideas "from here to here;" taking what I believe to be the best thinking and examples I've found in this industry and spreading them around. And finally, to offer you my own opinions, suggestions and viewpoints, developed from so many years' experiences.

You will find not one name of a specific, "real life" event anywhere in this book, except for the Boise River Festival, already noted as the case study for *Special Events: Inside and Out,* and projects noted in the section "about the author." I mention people by name only in the body copy when they are quote sources, book authors, etc. Except in one instance, none of them are directly connected to any events.

Use of such proper nouns would be unfair and would reduce the effective life of this book. Plans call for it to be available over several years, and during that time some events will become better (even great), while presently good ones may lose quality or die. To include them as specific examples as they stood at this writing could be unfair to them and to you when you return this book, which I hope you will, in the future.

OWNING UP

Let me emphasize at the outset that these contents are based *on my own* viewpoints, suggestions, concepts, opinions, appraisals and in many cases, ideas. They have been formed over three decades of experiencing more than 500 special events, encompassing virtually every type and size in a large number of geographic locations.

Some invited me to conduct deep-probe studies, as a means of offering plans from scratch for entirely new events or to make recommendations in existing ones for improvements. But a huge majority were those I studied personally, in the process of carrying out my many professional responsibilities with the Walt Disney organization, the United States Travel and Tourism Administration in the U.S. Department of Commerce, the John F. Kennedy Center for the Performing Arts, General Mills, Inc., and for a myriad of clients I serve in the capacity of an independent event consultant.

There were other times when my involvement came from an uncontrollable urge to study and analyze events, even though I went to a large number of them with my family, for the assumed purpose of "personal enjoyment." When you love events as I do, you are never able to turn off your analytical interest in them. Once an eventer, always an eventer!

Contents herein are my own. *But they are NOT the only ways to accommodate the subjects we'll cover.* Some have accused me of believing that, like a certain well-known performer's signature song, unless something was done *my way* it was not being done *the right way.* I do not for a moment feel that way.

I do believe fully in what I'm about to offer you in the following pages, or I wouldn't have included them. But others in the events industry feel just as strongly about their concepts and views as I do. And in many cases, there is a significant degree of disagreement between us. Since there are so few event absolutes – because event creation and production are not exact sciences—none of us are entirely right or wrong about a great many points; rather, we just have differing opinions.

NEGATIVE TO POSITIVE POLES

When you have finished this book, you may conclude that "this guy sure is a cynic; he wrote only about what's wrong with events." I'm not, really; it's just that I love events. You've perhaps seen the t-shirt captioned, "I Yell Only Because I Care." I'm figuratively wearing it as I write every word.

If I had composed this opus while using my Goody-Two-Shoes-Micro-very-Soft-hearted Windows® 95 word-processing system, you would have wasted your money on this book, or you simply wouldn't have bought it in the first place. Your learning curve would have taken a deep dip by the "they're-all-sooooo-really-cool" approach. It's easier to see (and you don't need very much help with) what's right. It's the pain-causing cavities that should be filled or pulled that concern us. I can only pray that my negatives will lead to positives.

Now let me snap into a new metaphor for a moment while chancing a Shakespearean observation that I ". . . protest too much, methinks." Generally you take your car to a mechanic for the purpose of finding out what's wrong with it and correcting its problems. You don't want a litany of what's right, especially not at the hourly charges of those experts these days.

I'm hoping that you seasoned eventers have come to this book for the same reasons in the events context, and that you entry-level folks want it to help stop problems before they get started. For those of you who are students of special events, my wish is for you to recognize and beware of more or less widespread weaknesses to enable you to play key roles in the constant improvement of event quality as you join us professionally on the margin of or into the first years of the new century.

POSITIONING PRONOUNS IN THE RESPONSIBLE CASE

Shunning custom, I plan to avoid use of the literary "we" in this work, as you may have already noticed. I find the I-really-mean-me "we" truly irritating, even when used by those granted, elevated, graduated, stealing or marrying into the "we" privilege—the royals, popes, editors or cloyingly-cheerful nurses ("Did *we* take *our* pills this morning?"). By using "I," I am declaring that these are my own thoughts, my own perceptions, my own perspectives, my own suggestions, my own feelings.

Conversely, since I'm addressing YOU, "you" will not be that impersonal person, "the reader." You are now and will remain YOU!

In order to fulfill my message mission, I will place you in differing positions from time to time in order to give you the most advantageous viewpoint for considering the subject at hand. In some cases, you may be a paid executive director or staff member. At other times, you might be a volunteer, either in an executive role or as an important staff person. On still other matters, you could be a spectator or in an audience. I have tried to make each of your positions obvious as you slip into it.

READING THE SAME LANGUAGE

Let me now define some terms I'll be using throughout the coming pages. Perhaps some of the following meanings can be challenged, but you and I must agree on meanings of certain terms *as they are used in this book,* or I'll be writing in one direction while you're reading in another. Not good.

Certainly the first term we should consider is the sum and substance of this entire book, so let's start with it.

SPECIAL EVENTS: As used herein—extraordinary, non-spontaneous, planned occurrences designed to entertain, inform or provide enjoyment and/or inspiration to audiences and/or spectators. Advocacy of a product, service, philosophy, message, or a group of such, may also be a characteristic. Events require the services and assistance of volunteers, and, to widely varying degrees, they must rely on financial support from sponsors.

Based on our definition here, "regular" baseball games, church services, theatrical presentations, amusement park programming, concerts, dinner parties and the like do not qualify for our upcoming discussions.

AUDIENCE: *(from a Latin derivative word meaning, "the act of listening"; ref: "audio")* — a group of people at a special event who are present primarily *to hear,* but also *to see,* as well as possibly *to interact* with, programs within that event.

SPECTATORS: *(from the Latin root word for "to look")* – a group of people at a special event who are there primarily *to see* a planned program, such as a parade, arena show, stadium or court game, etc. Again, interaction may be a built-in.

> *Even though spectators may hear music, loud-speaker announcements, etc., their basic goal is to see, to observe what's going on. An essential part of an audience experience is that it be heard AND seen. Admittedly, many people use these terms interchangeably. I don't and won't.*

EVENTERS: (my own new word, to fulfill a long-standing need) people directly involved in the conceptual, planning, implementation, operation or evaluation of any special event, either earning salaries or wages, or serving gratis as volunteers.

EVENTSORSHIP: (another new word from me) relating to or being in the state or condition of special events. ("Eventship" sounds awful. And "events *man*ship" is sexist . . .so it had to be "eventsorship." Take it or leave it.)

WHAT'S THE DIFFERENCE?

You may have already noticed—or you soon will—that this book does not look nor read like the typical how-to litany or the customary textbook. You'll find sentence fragments (guaranteed F's in any English class worthy of its name), unusual uses of ellipsis points (. . .) more white space than is ordinarily found on many printed pages, "undeveloped" paragraphs and other inclusions that fly in the face of formal English dicta.

I call this communications system "Power Writing," of which I'm one of the world's leading advocates. I'll have a fully detailed discussion of it in Chapter 4, but I thought I'd better own up early to these glaring violations of formal grammar and punctuation so that you would not read these first chapters believing I was grammar- and punctuation-challenged . . . or the victim of drive-by English.

WHEREFORE ART THOU?

More than likely, you thumbed through this book before really getting into it. And you probably noticed quickly that there are no photos nor drawings, only a couple of graphs and not any logos or other kinds of symbols. Bummer. "What's going on?," you ask. Low budget? No, here's why:

I will take to task some special events' publicist in Chapter 4 who did not accept my invitation for a long-lasting publicity opportunity, i.e., submitting photos of their happenings for use in this book. Sixty-one events were asked to provide photos, at no cost and with the promise of no value judgments on events or photography. Only three responded, requiring cancellation of my photos plans.

In "Owning Up" above, I . . . well . . . *owned up* to the majority of contents in this work being my own ideas, opinions, recommendations. So far as I know those mental images are difficult to photograph or to show on a grid or pie graph.

Suppose I had been able to draw my own concepts or to illustrate with photos or other graphics creative approaches to, perhaps, decorations, event site layouts, entertainment scheduling and the hundreds of other event elements we'll consider together in these seven chapters. I would have done you, the reader, a big disservice; I would have substituted *my* images for those *you* are supposed to create as a traveler though this book.

My whole purpose in preaching the *quality* sermon in these pages is to get *you* to do the thinking, the imaging, the imag*in*ing, the conceptualizing, the innovating. *YOU* are the one who will furnish your own "art" to illustrate the points in this book, as *you* perceive them.

Welcome, partner!

BY THE BOOKS

Although this book has been prepared to stand alone, it's far more effective when used as a fully-interrelated companion to *SPECIAL EVENTS: INSIDE & OUT SECOND EDITION.* (referenced as *SE:IO* henceforth) Steven Wood Schmader, founding Executive Director of the enormously successful (we say that immodestly; I designed it and he brought it into being) Boise River Festival and I wrote that book in 1990, using that festival as its pivotal case study.

This new work deals largely with significant details of event operational *tactics*, whereas *SE:IO* is a comprehensive study of overall operational *strategies*. Hopefully, together they will prove highly beneficial by providing a truly complete study for the serious professional, volunteer, student and/or wannabe eventer.

Periodically throughout this work, footnotes will refer to sections of *SE:IO* that expound far more significantly on that particular subject. Especially noteworthy is *SE:IO's* exhaustive attention to sponsorships, the financial glue of special events, which will become enormously more important as we move into the 21st Century. Strategies for marketing and organization are other significant contributions in *SE:IO,* considerably broadened in this book.

In still other cases, this newer book's purpose and scope do not call for attention to such important *SE:IO* subjects as event feasibility studies, existing events vs. created ones, the ideal selling formula, effective proposal preparation, event evaluation and budgeting.

And continuing its role as a useful adjunct, this book delves significantly into matters that did not, at the time, fall within the *SE:IO* scope. Included are event cosmetics, the importance of themes, maximum effective use of entertainment, toward more user-friendly positioning for events, working out organizational muscle spasms and miscellaneous individual hints for overall event improvement. Finally, *SPECIAL EVENTS: Making Them Fit in the 21st Century* includes sixteen core opportunities in a kind of Workshop on Paper (Chapter 1) format, which will definitely benefit from applications of knowledge gleaned from a study of *SE:IO.*

WHAT ARE YOU GOING TO READ ABOUT?

Categorizing special events can take many formulas. For us, our attention will be on *the scope* of events, of which there are generally eight groupings:

1. Neighborhood Events   A gathering or program put on by a homeowners association, local merchants group, perhaps a church or a school; usually quite limited in terms of budget, reach, programmatic offerings, etc.

2. Community Events   Those whose reach-of-interest expands to several neighborhoods, up to and including suburban satellite cities or quasi-cities in the forms of named areas (such as "the Sunset District"). These may include food-named festivals, commemoration of historic events, amateur athletic competitions, and so on.

3. Metro Area Events   Those whose operational and appeal encompass several contiguous cities, communities and neighborhoods, often called a "Metropolitan Statistical Area" (MSA) in marketing. Most often, these events include large family-oriented festivals, musical offerings, major athletic competitions, historically- or geographically-themed happenings (Civil War episodes; those centering around rivers, lakes), etc.

4. Statewide Events   Obviously, those aimed at involving the entire state. A primary example is the celebration of a state's 100th anniversary of statehood, but there are others, primarily political, social, educational and professional in nature.

5. Regional Events   Ordinarily, statewide events broadened and clustered by contiguous states; often the link between state and national categories.

6. National Events   We're a nation that thinks B-I-G. Proof? Consider the mega-numbers of huge national events that have combined to become a major multi-billion-dollar industry. Convention bureaus barely mask open warfare in vying for those dollars. Among the monoliths: party political conventions, along with those centering on civic, fraternal, religious, sports, educational, artistic, labor, medical, individual business/professional, hobby and avocational, law enforcement, military and naval, beauty, fitness, charities, lifestyle, collectibles and other common interests.

7. International Events   Of course, sports leads the list here, but there are many other very important ones, for example, those dealing with global health, social, political, religious and economic issues.

8. Promotional Events   This is a hybrid category, born from the mating of any of the above classifications with a commercial promotion of a product or service. There is a difference between (A) promotional events and (B) sponsored events:

(A) is designed specifically and *primarily* to be a sales vehicle with the other event add-ons to attract more attention, appeal more widely to media, and often a commercial atmosphere; most frequently, a single company will cause the promotional event to be created and implemented, although product or company partners may be brought in when multiple joint marketing is deemed advisable; the sell need is primary, the event need is to serve as an important secondary support;

(B) is in one of the first seven categories above, with usually more than one sponsor participating as a means of subsidizing the event while focusing public attention on their product or services; generally, the event itself is the "visible first purpose," the sell aspect usually being the "timid" secondary (but still very important) and more subtle. They do involve audiences or spectators, but not always volunteers. However, for our purposes here, we shall include volunteerism as an ingredient.

Because the largest number of regularly engaged volunteers, especially, and of paid personnel in the U.S. events industry are and will likely continue to be engaged primarily in (2) Community and (3) Metro Area Events, these two categories are the pivots on which this book *primarily* (but not solely) spins. It's my fullest expectation that those of you interested or involved in the remaining five, with some obvious retuning here and there, will also find considerable value in these pages.

FITNESS AS A THEME

Without much of an analogical stretch, special events can be likened to our bodies. Both have arms, legs, heads, torsos, internal organs, etc., and every one of those parts have distinct purposes. To function efficiently—even if nothing more than to avoid atrophy—each human and event body part must perform the tasks for which it was designed. Neglect through lack of use or abuse can cause malfunction of any part, very often laming the whole organism.

Everybody knows it's wise to have a thorough physical before starting any fitness program. That applies to events as well. Let's adjust our rhetorical stethoscopes and get our imaginary tongue depressors held just so while I try to show you how to be an "event physician."

Even if you're not yet in this field, you should learn *now* what to look for in an event examination. You'll be surprised how this knowledge will help you keep unhealthy conditions from developing, or assist you in uncovering them if they get by you and start afflicting your event.

HERE'S YOUR EVENT EXAM CHART

√   Important: check the blood condition.

   Does it need a new infusion?

   Is the pressure so low that the patient is sluggish?

   Is hypertension caused by the stress of internal conflicts?

√   Determine whether the patient suffers from arrested growth.

√   Test: does one hand know what the other is doing?

√   Eye exam: Do the eyes look ahead?

   Are they closed to reality too much of the time?

   Is there a focus, or is the event going in all directions at once?

√   Carefully check hearing: do the ears hear only what they want to hear?

√   Is the basic bone structure strong enough, or do you need some splints?

√   Is there a plague called "Virulent Ownership" endangering this event?

√   Does the patient have fun, or is existence a real drag?

Each positive diagnosis multiplies the need for a good, solid— perhaps even strenuous—event fitness program. And even if your event is well toned, it needs to be kept that way, possibly through a change in exercise programming. Constant reexamination is imperative; there really is wisdom in having a regular physical.

Enough warm-up. Now let's get on with our event fitness program!

Notes

[1]It's not within the mission of this book to try to define "family," one of the sensitive issues of the 1990s, which will likely have an extended life well into the 2000s. Rather, "family" used herein refers solely to an all-age group, general-interest," wholesome" programming span at an event or a gated *entertainment park.*

Chapter One

WORKOUT ON PAPER

Before we get into heavy exercising, we need to limber up our creative muscles, but not with barbells or machines. We'll use a brick. That's right, A brick. Just one.[1]

An ordinary red brick will do, the kind measuring about eight inches long, three or so inches wide, and a little over two inches thick, weighing somewhere in the neighborhood of four pounds. You'll also need a pen and writing paper.

Now, look at that brick long and hard. Really study it. (You might want to do this alone, so that no one will see you staring at a common brick for any length of time. Image, you know.)

Okay, now write down as many ways as your imagination will whisper to you for the use of that one brick. Sorry, you can't multiply it and build a city.

To help turn on your creativity, let me suggest a first answer: your brick can be used as a doorstop. Perhaps a little more imaginative suggestions: it can also be used as a paperweight, for linear measurement (lay the brick end-over-end), to estimate weight (compare something with its four pounds), etc. Now it's your turn; with a socially acceptable response, tell me what you can do with that brick.

_____

_____

_____

_____

_____

Okay, time's up. Were you surprised at how many ways a single brick can be put to use, over and above those for which it seemed intended? Remember that brick as we move through this book. I hope it will spur you to search for other ways to do something other than the one(s) that come to mind first or which seem to be your only options.

> **Always look for new and different but better ways of doing new things,** as well as fresh, unique, pleasantly surprising applications or combinations for existing ones. Regardless of suggestions or recommendations I make throughout this book, you are expected to consider, deal with or recreate each entirely differently from, but better than, their usual or expected formats or looks. In your plans, pet shows, arts and craft fairs, parades—**EVERYTHING!**—should not look or be exactly like any other of its kind on earth.

My hope also is that you'll always remember it as you move through your participation in the special events industry, which is sorely and always in need of fresh, creative, innovative thinking and applications.

Many may oppose liberalism in politics and government. When it comes to the nature of special events and their publicly displayed components, however, there is plenty of room—always a big hearty welcome—for liberal thinkers. Of course, fiscal conservatives are nice to have around for budgeting and expenditure control. In every really successful event, you'll find the two working very well together, with verbal scrapes every now and then, of course.

AND NOW FOR THE *REAL* WORKOUT

Briefly described on the following pages are sixteen observances, happenings, opportunities, occasions, etc., some of which actually exist, or did at one time. Other fictional ones are designed to provide you with fun topics, but they just might become real events some day.

They are meant to be used in a workshop context and format as subjects for which exercises can be developed through encounters with each forthcoming chapter.

Ideally, to maximize use of this workout-on-paper concept, you should select and stay with just one of the following sixteen case studies from the outset. That chosen core profile can be layered with each chapter's suggestions or products of its generated creativity, resulting in a well-structured, thoroughly fleshed-out, high-quality event framework by book's end.

Option: You may substitute your own event concept or an event that is actually in existence in your locale for this application. Regardless, the purpose of choosing a subject is to build a fully complete workshop-calibre case study.

If you decide to work on an existing event, assume for our purposes here that it has yet to happen. See how well you can distance yourself from its reality to help you find new ways to improve it.

YOU WILL HAVE FUN!

Although these exercises are meant to produce important, serious and practical results, they're also meant to be very enjoyable. If you do not really have fun working in this manner, especially on this subject, perhaps you should consider some other career or volunteer opportunity more suited to your personality.. Special events is not a field for everyone, especially the sober. (Not *that* kind of sober; I mean super-serious, somber, subdued, quiet, sedate, dull, blah.)

Some of the following sixteen cases may be difficult subjects for a full-effort operational program; they are intended to be learning experiences by being formidable mental and creative challenges. Others are deceptive; they appear to be barely challenging or even no-brainers, but don't be fooled. Both categories require careful study before developing a creative, maximum-potential program practical enough to become successful reality. Taking an easy way out with "the expected" will only produce just another cookie-cutter event that will assuredly serve without any distinction whatsoever, for itself or you.

Bottom-line budgets are offered only as some kind of workable parameter and to rein in on any recklessly out-of-control thinking. In these allocations, there is no allowance for profits, since nearly all events are not for profit. All given funds are to be used for planning and implementation. Important: we're assuming no admission charges, relying instead on adequate sponsorship dollars to carry the event. Despite some expressions to the contrary, I believe a well-sponsored, no-admission-cost event is not only highly desirable, but will become the standard in the 21st Century.

Space considerations will not permit presentation of every salient detail that might fully flesh out concepts. When this book is used in a teaching format, you instructors may wish to add your own details to make projects more meaningful, workable, interesting, and better suited to the immediate community. You may also enlarge or reduce budgets, change timing, subtract details, move venues to familiar ones in your local area, etc.

Speaking of details, if you do not handle them well—if you do not have a hefty appetite for dealing with countless but important fine points—then I suggest that you seek a less detail-oriented pursuit, like perhaps neurosurgery, child-raising, theoretical physics or (heaven help you!) celestial mechanics.

IT'S TIME FOR THE RFP

You are about to meet a device most professional eventers face at least once in their lives. You are blessed; you will encounter it many times before you complete this book. Or you should, if effective and retentive learning is your goal.

Say hello for the first time to the "Request for Proposal," our industry's redoubtable "RFP." It's a document prepared by those needing or wanting a specific type, a specially tailored events, constructed for their own unique needs.

Your repeated RFP rendezvous will come as you complete each chapter. You will want to turn back to this unit, select that/those portions of information and its response segments that apply to what you've just studied. You will then want to fill out your detailed recommendations in appropriate response segments.

By the time you've completed this book, hopefully you will find that you have put together a wonderfully comprehensive, exciting, total-concept plan for your selected case study or equally pleasing recommendations for improving an your chosen existing event. My hope is that you will surprise yourself by developing a remarkably creative, fresh and very practical overall plan.

There is no set, across-the-board RFP and response formats. Rather, they're written compilations of specifications, expectations, desires, dreams, objectives, budget and fiscal guidelines, resources, sponsor goals and general background information. If it's properly thought out and prepared, the RFP can lead you, as respondent, to create on paper a complete, meaningful and workable project summary plan.

RFPs are almost always issued to more than one recipient for bidding purposes. Each respondent, therefore, should rightly consider himself/herself in competition with other professionals and should be prepared to compete successfully by fashioning the finest, most complete, best thought-out, most workably creative and imaginative plan possible—especially after having read my books!

This widely used instrument, if it is well-designed, tells you exactly what the issuer wants and what's expected of you in the response. Nearly always, there's a dated deadline, which frequently gives you less time than you'd like to complete your investigations and responses. So be prepared to move!

Your objective upon receiving an RFP should be to design responses that surpass those expectations and minimum specifications. Except the given dollar amounts. Unless that issuer has left that fact open for consideration, you should stick strictly to it. An open-budget RFP nearly always means the issuer doesn't know how much the project will cost, asking you to suggest an amount and very frequently to outline details where you think money will come from and the strategy for getting it.

Interestingly, application of the RFP format and its basic objectives work surprisingly well for events already in existence. Therefore, if you are involved with a standing event, you can prepare your own RFP and "address it to yourself." It will become an effective means for spotlighting strengths and laying bare weaknesses, a process that can be particularly worthwhile if those RFP responses are used to improve the health and vitality of your event.

Do not let the following RFPs frighten you. I introduce them early in our journey to serve as maps showing us where we're going and to call out what you should be looking for along the way. And who knows? One day, this practice experience may help you prepare and issue your own world-class RFP or guide you in evaluating candidate responses.

MAKING YOUR RFP INFORMATION FIT

From the outset of my efforts to devise or collect and then present workshop case studies, my primary objective has been to offer an especially wide range of projects. Not only would this span increase the probability of my hitting your hot-buttons with one or more of these case; I also wanted to illustrate, even if on a limited scale, the extraordinary variances in the types of special events.

But that goal was burdened with it its own inherent problem: it would be impossible to put together a set of working guidelines and judgmental criteria whose every dimension and detail would be perfect fits for every case study. For example, at least one out of the sixteen, and very often more than one, would be out of kilter—just not in sync—with the others, in terms of best time of year for presentation targeted number of visitors (some would be hugely successful with a few hundred, others would require hundreds of thousands to be considered a front-runner), appropriate event duration, etc.

I have opted for variety over uniformity, which means I must offer you a generous amount of latitude in adapting elements of your selected case study to the broad-based list of RFP specifications.

To make this whole concept work, I had to provide some sort of common starting point, and the list below is it. If your choice won't fit one or more of these criteria, so be it, but unless your omission or alteration is brightly obvious, be prepared to defend your action.

RFP Starting Points

Location: all involved metro areas have a resident population of at least 300,000

Number of Event Visits: 400,000-600,000, actual

Event Duration: seven days—five weekdays, one weekend

Seasonal Span: warm months only

Planning Period: your event happens at least one full year from "now"

RFP COMPONENTS FOR ALL PROJECTS

You should start this study by carefully reading and going over every detail of the sixteen case studies outlined in an RFP format designed for workshop use. Take your time; really get to know each one. Then select the one that interests you most. Use of this strategy suggests that you stick with your first selection throughout this book.

I have given you my proposed event needs in each RFP paragraph beneath its numbered title. If a needed element comes to mind in the process of considering responses, however, develop and work under your own assumptions, but state clearly what they are and how you justify them.

IN YOUR RFP RESPONSE, YOU SHOULD:

1. **Provide a selection of three audience/spectator/media/sponsor-magnetizing, catchy names for your project**—ones you feel will be effectively promotable and do a thorough job of describing its concept. As you evaluate your ideas, remember that the name must wear well over a number of years and, when obvious, in various geographic locations. Link each suggested name with your reasoning, i.e. why you chose those you're suggesting. Assume that I, as the RFP issuer, will make the final choice.

2. **Specify exactly by dates the seven-day period you're recommending**—give reasons if it differs from the suggested five-weekdays/one-weekend criterion. Bear in mind that your selected event, if it's an annual or semiannual occurrence, will happen very close to the stated time every year. If your selection is keyed to move to or be reproduced in other areas, take those other seasonalities into account.

Therefore, even though your outside southern venue might work well in November or March, that timing will most likely not be well suited to the American tundra. Generally, mid-April through mid-October should be your preferred operational span. Remember, weather doesn't impact only outdoor events. A blizzard or monsoon is nearly as disagreeable to indoor-event-goers because they have to endure those nasty conditions during vehicular round-trips, parking, and walking to and from indoor venues.

3. **Give details of the site(s) you would recommend and why.** Prepare a written description and a map of the event as it would be laid out on that site, along with an overall map indicating its location vis-à-vis your metro area. Don't worry about the possibly unpolished outcome of your drawings; we're seeking event talent, not cartographic excellence.

4. **Include the best entertainment lineup you can provide,** with a seven-day daily performance timetable. Also give the types (and names, if you have them or can develop your own) of performers who will contribute to your chosen theme, and indicate the number of stages (confirming to the site map above) or other non-stage locations and where each soloist or group will perform.

5. **Present types of displays, entertainment, games, and other activities you can recruit or create** that will assure maximum interaction with visitors of your demographic profile. Interaction—the actual audience/spectator involvement, in which people overtly "do something," if they choose to do so—is one of the distinguishing capabilities that set special events apart from most other forms of entertainment. It's a virtual certainty that visitor interaction will become increasingly important in Century 21.

6. **Present your concepts for the opening and the closing events**—ceremonies, celebrations, special shows . . . programming that will give it a spirited, high-action kick-off and a closing that will leave your constituency begging for more. Remember: your big ending show can be your first sponsor and attendance promotional effort for the coming year.

7. I have given a suggested theme in each of my sixteen RFPs below, but you should feel entirely free to adopt and recommend one of your own for your chosen case. If you want to impress me as the issuer, you might even offer more than one. **In any case, explain how you plan to weave that theme into every element of this event**—decorations, entertainment, signage, programming—everything. For our needs here, I'm recommending a strong purist approach to theme usage, purposely overextending these applications in order to demonstrate their capabilities, applicabilities and important cosmetic contributions.

8. **Using your fertile imagination, describe in reasonable details the highly creative decorations** you recommend that I use on site and in the surrounding metro area to promote or enhance this event, and indicate where and in what patterns you would place those decorations. Remember: *theme.*

9. **Formulate a reasonably detailed organizational plan describing all needed committees,** their specific duties and jurisdictional areas, and a reasonable estimate of the number of volunteers you feel would be needed for each. Include a brief innovative volunteer recruiting strategy, as well as a proposed administrative structure (number and position description for any paid staff members you suggest).

10. **Outline in sufficient detail a marketing plan** that has two divisions, a major one aimed at the local market, and a secondary one intended eventually for your regional or national scene (your choice). Include a media release, fact sheet and media advisory aimed at maximizing media attention to and during opening day, closing day and any other outstanding offerings you can make media-worthy to assist me in building attendance and enticing sponsors.

11. In most instances, I have provided you with a block of funds, but you'll need to raise more bucks. **Draw up a strategy for attracting at least six additional sponsors** (give types or, if you have them, specific names) who will provide the remaining dollars, indicating why you chose each, what your plan offers them and how much funding you expect each to provide.[2]

12. Don't worry about creating a line-item budget. **Use the bottom-line figure as a guide in determining the size, scope and impact of your chosen project.** In a real RFP response, you would be expected to provide such a detailed budget. Important note: money is always short in the events industry. More frequently than might be expected, when really good ideas of large dimensions clearly worth the money are developed, funding can be very often be found. If not, big concepts can usually be re-shaped to fit snug dollar collars. However, the purpose of this Workshop on Paper is to get you to think creatively—and big!

As stated above, there is no standard format for an RFP. That's also true for an RFP response. However, the one I'm formulating below meets most of the RFP response needs. If each of your responses is well enough fleshed-out, several will require several word-processed or long-hand-written pages.

For quick back-and-forth references, parenthetical chapter numbers refer to the book location that will relate in detail to that subject.

REQUEST FOR PROPOSAL RESPONSE OUTLINE

1. Your name and position (give yourself a really cool title):

2. Organization you represent (from case study or make up your own):

3. Number and name of the case event you have chosen or the name of some other event you prefer to study:

4. Three suggested titles for the new event or to replace the existing one:

5. Inclusive days and dates you recommend for this event – and your reasoning (Chapter 7):

6. In reasonable detail, describe the theme you have chosen, supporting that description with your reasons; for more satisfaction (yours and mine), offer some really creative surprises (Chapter 3):

7. Describe the location(s) in the chosen metro area(s); provide it in writing, giving your rationale for its/their selection; support with drawn map(s) (Chapter 7):

8. Describe the specific layout of the event on that/those sites, showing all elements and their locations; provide a map "translation" of your descriptions; defend your selection(s) with reasons (why tents are so located, stages placed, food areas selected, parking lots positioned, etc.) (various chapters):

9. Present in detail your recommendations for entertainment – names or types; add to the effectiveness and strength of your plan by coming up with interesting names of soloists or groups (Chapter 2):

10. Provide a detailed, hour-by-hour schedule of musical and non-musical entertainment, noting where each will appear; remember the importance of pacing your event through carefully scheduled entertainment (Chapter 2).

11. Develop a detailed, hour-by-hour schedule of special attractions, which in some cases may not require stages; use short phrases to describe their presentations; again, attention-getting names will enrich your recommended program appeal (Chapter 2):

12. Describe in full your plans for decorations and where they will be used; provide artwork, even if it might not be represent high artistic talent, to help present your concepts as clearly as possible Chapter 3):

13. Using information from the RFP paragraph and adding any additional ideas you might have on his topic, show how you plan to put plenty of "heart" in your event (Chapter 5):

14. Carefully and in sufficient detail, present your entire grid for an organization you feel would be required to implement your plans; prescribe how you will recruit volunteers with a creative program; name committees, telling what each will do and the approximate number of volunteers you will need for each and creating a brief Position Description for each of those volunteers and Committee Description for each unit of volunteers (Chapter 6):

15. Create a full-blown marketing plan for your event; include specific publicity approaches and document samples; decide whether you'll use advertising, and if so, note in what manner you will fund it; aim most of that plan to your immediate community, but include at least a reasonably fleshed-out approach for "going regional" or "national" (Chapter 4):

16. Suggest concept for creative forms of food and equally creative forms of merchandise that will both increase income and contribute to the enjoyment quotient of my event, it's theme, etc.; recommend use of script or cash for food and state your reasons; give your rationale in suggesting that your event sell or not sell alcoholic beverages (Chapters 2 & 7):

17. There are two events already being presented in this metro area that you feel would make ideal adjuncts to your new one. "Create" these events with short written descriptions and provide a strategy for folding them into your new one, thus strengthening your event and benefiting those former stand-alones (Chapter 7):

18. I have strong reason to believe that there may be some political and law enforcement resistance to the introduction of this new event. Describe their objections, now that you've investigated this matter, and provide a strategy for surmounting this hurdle (Chapter 7):

19. Now carefully review all recommendation and descriptions in the RFP response. Put down anything your creativity can come up with that I missed in my RFP that will really improve my planned project – and incidentally, cause me to choose your response-plan over all others from competitors:

20. Summarize reasons for your strong confidence in your overall plan, why you believe it will be highly successful and will meet or surpass every goal of my RFP. In short, sell your plan.

AND NOW TAKE YOUR PICK FROM MY RFPS

1. Festival Under Fire

THEME: "Fires of Friendship." "Good" uses of fire—campfires, torch runs, cook-outs, glass-shaping, ceramics production and similar hobbies, etc. What other positive uses can you think of for the fire theme and how can you incorporate them into this event? If you want to replace this theme, state your reasons for your choice.

I represent an amalgam of organizations representing fire-fighters, fire-prevention industries (manufacturers of smoke-alarms, extinguishers, etc.) and insurance companies that have formed a consortium to support an annual seven-day festival of major proportions, having a fire theme.

They have dual purposes in doing so: (1) to promote safety by making people more conscious of the importance of fire uses and prevention; and (2) to expand awareness of the significant roles fire-fighters and "anti-fire" companies and their programs play in everyday life. Although they don't want to diminish the importance and seriousness of these two messages, they want this event to be a great deal of fun and very interactive with the thousands of visitors it is expected to draw.

Your city is one of twelve that has received my RFP, and the municipal powers that be are determined to host this festival, which could have an impact of $15 million on the local economy. Estimated initial donation: $1 million; you need to raise another $250,000 from sponsors. Please let me have your highly detailed RFP response. And make it a winner.

2. Stars, Stripes And Fun Forever

THEME: "America's Most Patriotic Festival." What can you do to make every element truly American? Emphasized: EVERY element. Do you have another patriotic theme idea you like better for this event? What is it—and why substitute it for the one given?

Your city, through a group of community leaders, has decided to host a major July 4th festival, which they want to become the premiere annual event in that area. But they demand that it be "different but better" (where've you seen that before?) than the thousands of other Independence Day observances all over the country.

They want it to be unique and enticing enough to swell midsummer tourism to their city by at least one-third during its third year. Through donations and the projected sale of sponsorships, they expect to give you $1.5 million; another $375,000 must come from sponsors you'll line up. Other than that, they haven't another clue as to what that event would need, its length, its unique characteristics, etc.

It's all up to you . . . and if you don't have especially large amounts of fun coming up with an RFP response for me on this one, may your fireworks fizzle!

3. Games People Will Play

THEME: "Sports Things." How can you use implements required for sports as wall decorations, planters, table centerpieces and every other way you can imagine? There may be a far better sports theme in your own creative cells, which you may certainly use in place of this one, but tell why.

A collection of wealthy, civic-minded sports enthusiasts in your city wants to develop an all-inclusive amateur sports festival. They've asked me to issue this RFP, emphasizing that they want it to appeal to males and females, to all age categories and to those at every economic level.

Fortunately, your metro area possesses some of the finest athletic facilities in the state, designed for every major sport, but they've never been properly nor effectively (and certainly not fully) utilized. All of these facilities have pledged their full support for this project, agreeing to host events for expenses only, no fees. Long-range plans call for this annual festival to become national in scope, but for openers, they'll be happy with a solid regional draw.

Through several grants, projected income from concessions and merchandise sales, backing from a number of local institutions, and hefty sponsorship income predicted, this self-appointed "sports commission" has set a budget of $1 million.

Because of your reputation as an enormously successful event designer, producer and sponsorship salesperson, I fully expect you to create the most original, unique and successful regional amateur sports festival in the nation. Oh, yes, you have to arrange another $250,000 from sponsors. Let me have that strategy and a full cache of great ideas in your RFP response.

4. Event Make-Over

THEME: "River of Many Happy Returns." What things that are related to the river can you use to emphasize in every way the return of the festival to its original theme and purpose? Is there another river theme you like better? Use it—but tell why.

Your city has hosted a metrowide event, called "Riverfest," every summer since 1964.

As so often happens with aging events, Riverfest has gradually floated away from its original name-theme; it now has very little relationship to the river. It has been more than a decade since its staff and volunteers have added any substantial new element to this event, which spreads itself over four weeks and fifty-seven venues with many miles separating several of those venues. Last year a senior badminton competition was introduced; it attracted fewer than fifty players and about the same number of spectators. "Riverfest" honchos claim 700,000 visits annually, which *must* include 500,000 phantoms.

Through a cleverly planned, devious but welcome *coup´ d'état´*, a group of "radical liberals" have finally seized control of the board of directors and are determined to build a whole new festival right on top of the very tired, worn-out, weary, out-of-sorts version. They do want to keep its name while building events and occasions that, in fact, center around the river.

I am contacting you, asking you to develop this make-over, no holds barred. Your concepts in your RFP response, please. Oh yes, they'll give you an operational sum of $2.5 million to help you work your miracle, but you'll have to get sponsors to toss in another $500,000.

5. Planning Religiously

THEME: "In Perfect Harmony." How can you use musical items—instruments, sheet music, actual music being played, etc.—to create this theme? Or do you have in mind another religious theme you prefer? If so, use it, but do tell why in your RFP response.

Churches, synagogues and other religious organizations in your metro area have entered into a consortium to design and sponsor a city-wide, seven-day event aimed at attracting all age groups, but with several elements having an especially strong appeal to teens and low-age adults.

Its purpose is to reverse the pervasive perception, primarily among the young, that religion is "out of it"—dull, boring, not valid today, made up only of tired clichés, etc.—it's anything but enjoyable or meaningful.

What on earth—or in heaven's name—can you do in your RFP response to me, that hasn't been done already? Bake sales, gift bazaars, car-washes, potluck dinners, bingo competitions, carnivals, mother-daughter/father-son banquets? Sure, you might want to do all of these—*but don't you dare do them the "usual," very tired ways!* Find entirely new approaches; for example, find an incredible, colorful, really unexpected location for your selection and truly imaginative decorations—all chosen to play perfectly to the younger adult crowd.

Remember the brick! You want to do things that are also entirely new, different, highly appealing, but still wholesome, that will really focus—or refocus—attention on religion as a viable, relevant, actually enjoyable force in today's world.

Summary: in short, how can you make religion cool? Their budget tops out at $400,000; they'll give you $200,000, but you'll have to come up with the remainder through sponsorships. Think BIG and pray even bigger. Then let me have your RFP response.

6. Golf For a Change

THEME: "Slices of the Old and the New." How can you use golf "things"—old photos with new holograms, old fashioned wearing apparel with the latest styles, ancient equipment with the most modern, etc.? If you like, come up with a golf theme of your own, with a rationale, of course.

You have a good chance of being hired as its executive director by the Metropolitan Open Golf Experience (MOGE) tournament and festival, about to enter its tenth year of existence. You're a strong candidate for the job primarily because of the exceptional level of creativity you demonstrated during your job interviews.

Its board told you that their event just doesn't seem to be going anywhere . . . it's become "just another golf competition" in an obvious decline, and they want you to do something about that.

Although the golf tournament is its centerpiece, the festival part needs just as much attention; it demands a spate of activities that will appeal to the golfer and to the non-golfing public. Despite its stagnant state, this entire event still attracts enough sponsorship dollars to support a total operating cost of $1 million (not including prize money), down from twice that amount just three years ago.

Change is what's needed and wanted. Here's your opportunity to take a zestless regional golf tournament, along with its festival, and make this event stand out over and above all others. Oh, yes. *You* have to raise the prize money! How much will you need to make this a truly attractive tournament and where will you get those bucks?

Your potential employers are awaiting your RFP response through me before deciding on you for that cushy big-bucks job. Do your best.

7. Bouquets to the Winners

THEME: "The Avant-Garde*ner*" How will you recommend to the garden club that this theme be implemented to emphasize the most up-to-date methods, equipment and materials used in gardening today? Even some far-out approaches should be considered. If you prefer, develop your own garden theme idea—and tell why you prefer it.

ISGC—the Intercontinental Society of Garden Clubs—has asked me to send an RFP to your city's special events department relative to holding its huge (and very locally lucrative) annual convention in your city.

There are ten metro areas in the world receiving this document, but your city is the only one in the USA. This event always attracts worldwide media coverage, so it angles the tourism spotlight right squarely in your area.

City shakers are determined to bag this event trophy and have raised $1 million for costs to host it; ISCG will toss in another $500,000, but another $370,000 must be raised from sponsorships. By you.

Named to head up the event's local task force, you are determined to give them the freshest, most creative, all-encompassing, dynamic, workable plan the ISGC has ever had. What are its elements, and where will you get the sponsorship dollars? I'll expect a dynamite RFP response.

8. Words About a Festival About Words

THEME: Challenge: Just try building a festival—an interesting and fun one keyed to the English language! Presented here for illustration is one based on some of our most over-worked communication crutches: *the trite, stale, banal, clichéd words or phrases.*

Your city has been asked to design a thematic, especially interesting, truly unusual and fun-laced, festival-type, public adjunct to the annual convention of the American Guild of Writers, Editors, Columnists, Copy-writers and Journalists, reduced to an easily handled (?) "AGWECCJ." Because this 17,000-member group uses the English language, American style, as its primary work tool, it seems creatively appropriate to reflect the importance of our language.

In a brainstorming session conducted to start your response to my RFP, you called together a greatly respected group of creative thinkers, who convinced you to settle on poking fun by tangling with The Language. You've collected a list of them, some of which you have already affixed to event elements, but you need to fill out your plans with *many* other exciting offerings.

Expect to spend $1 million, $250,000 is yet to be raised through sponsorships from ???

Here's some early planning, but this is barely a beginning. You have to fill up seven days with wonderful things. What will they be? (By the way, if you can create a totally different concept and theme, which you think will do a better job of representing AGWECCJ, throw out the following and start anew with yours, along with your rationale.) Make everything you include truly different from the expected.

THEME NAME	EVENT ACTIVITY OR FACILITY
Just a Stone's Throw	Team competition, writers vs. the public; who can throw stones farthest
Some Assembly Required	(My nomination for the most vicious and terrifying phrase in the English language.) Adults compete in a child's building system contest
At the End of Your Rope	Tug-of-war
Cut to the Chase	Relay race
Bag and Baggage	Competition; who can carry the greatest number of articles the farthest distance in the shortest time
But You Can't Have Your Cake and Eat It, Too	Cake-eating contest
You Have My Word	Vote on the most beautiful, ugliest, etc. words in the English language (results can garner high media appeal)
Bag of Tricks	Magician performances
Jump to Conclusions	Hurdles competition or pole vaulting
At Your Beck and Call	Communications system
A Lot on Your Plate	Food court
That's Beside the Point	Dart-throwing competition
Bet Your Bottom Dollar	Sit-down Bingo
Necessity's the Mother of Invention Area	Portable toilets
Dressed to the Nines	Fashion show
Bite Off More than You Can Chew	Bubble-gum blowing competition
Blessings in Disguise	Masquerade parade
Bright Eyed and Bushy Tailed	Pet show
Go By (Buy) the Book	Books sale
Outta Sight!	Lost and found
Face Up to It	Children's face-painting
Without Further A-Do	Opening ceremonies or program
After All's Said and Done	Closing ceremonies or program

Now move right along with your RFP response by *giving visitors much more to do.*

9. Lost and Found Hours Celebration

THEME: Here is an example in which the very purpose and name of the event is its de facto theme. If you can, however, have a go at developing other alternate highly creative theme wording.

So far as I know at this writing, no truly *significant* events exist in this nation that capitalize and hinge on these two biannual occurrences, yet virtually every person is impacted by them—big time!

Daylight Saving Time begins at 2:00 a.m. every first Sunday in April and Standard Time returns at 2:00 a.m. on October's final Sunday. (Some locales are exempted.)

Think of ways to use this theme during one or both change-over periods for a fun celebration, which also happens to remind people to change their clocks ("spring forward, fall back" an hour). Important beneficial by product: it can also remind everyone to install or check smoke and CO_2 detectors at home and work, a reminder the media are sure to love. Estimated entire cost: $150,000 per observance, one in April, one in October, of which you must raise $37,500 for each observance.

POSSIBILITY: Think about using the overall theme of "time" to broaden your options and expand your opportunities . . . and make your event really memorable. (You may use the time theme example in Chapter Three, but you must greatly expand that concept and make it RFP friendly.)

(IMPORTANT: This is the only selection from the sixteen that is not predicated on a seven-day event; each observance should take place Wednesday, Thursday, Friday, and Saturday.)

10. National Condom Week[3]

THEME: "Condom Wisdom," "Being in Control," or another you may find more appealing and/or more suited to your community. Occasions can't always be easy to deal with, and here's one that definitely isn't.

This observance takes place annually, February 14-21 (fixed timing; notice that it's not during warm months), and its stated purpose is "to educate consumers, patients, students and professionals on the prevention of sexually transmitted diseases, especially AIDS, and teenage pregnancies."

What can you do in your community annually to get people involved in this mission . . . to get the public spotlight focused on it through one or more captivating, entirely tasteful, serious but attractive and entertaining events?

This concept offers an example for those who prefer to render a significant service in an engrossing, weighty, arresting fashion. It requires a tightrope-walk between The Serious and The Flippant, between Too Light and Too Dark—a different but highly rewarding challenge.)

Total projected cost: $250,000; you need to raise $62,500 of that amount from sponsors. An amalgam of condom manufacturers and health-related organizations have issued an RFP and you got one. What's your winning response?

11. Earth Day*

THEME: Select from such concepts as "Now! It's Your Turn," "The "*U*" in F*Uture*," "There's Only One World," or come up with your own, one that promises to render a better plan. Observed each April 22nd "to reclaim the purity of the air, water and living environment."

Your assignment: It has been determined that this occasion needs a lot of pumping up. It's lost much of its strength in recent years, and the Environmental Protection Agency, using private contributions, issued an RFP, through me, one going to you. I'm asking you to design a seven-day program, ending on Earth Day, for your metro area—one that will, in fact, revitalize this observance.

Another major goal: to win over those who are totally indifferent to the future of the environment. EPA's specifications say that they want your plan to be a prototype—one so successful that it can be duplicated in major metro areas throughout the nation a year following yours. What is your plan for a total cost of $500,000?

(This is one of only two selections of the sixteen cases not requiring additional funding from sponsorships. This one also has a fixed final date of observance.)

12. The Great American Money Festival

THEME: Again, it's name is its theme: *money*. How we earn it, how it's produced, its history, interesting stories involving money, staggering money statistics, etc. Note that it's time to remind people to pay their income taxes. If you prefer, come up with an entirely different money-related theme.

Can you make a fun event out of this annual income tax tear-jerker? If you're plenty creative, you can.

Speaking of money, the National Society of Tax Yaks (N.A.S.T.Y) is picking up half the tab on this one event; projected cost: $500,000 for development and implementation; you raise $250,000 of it.

They have issued an RFP through me, and I have sent you one. As you might expect, they want to promote further use of accountants, tax specialists and tax lawyers by the public. Remember to see how many no-cost activities you can find: free displays by the U.S. Mint, banking associations, coin collectors, even the IRS.

Your event may be more or less than the seven-day indication above, depending on what day the April 15 tax deadline falls, which should be the final, grand day of your event.

For sponsors to make up your other funding, try handlers of aspirin, upset stomach medicines, high-blood pressure controllers, makers of headache powders, scratch pads, calculators, and others related to money, mathematics, taxes, etc.

13. A Princely and Princessly Affair

THEME: "First Loves." How will you use the "first loves" (cars, jewels, etc., presented below) of Their Highnesses in clever but not far-fetched or in "over-done" taste? If you like, develop a theme along entirely different lines.

Their Royal Highnesses, the Crown Prince and Princess of an oil-rich, middle eastern kingdom, have been invited by the U.S. government to enjoy a seven-day tour of the United States. Its purpose is to bolster recently damaged relations between our government and theirs, so a really special, good and safe experience every moment must be assured.

As the State Department protocol official in charge of their visit, you must plan their itinerary and their activities at each stop.

You have learned that His Highness is an ardent big-game hunter, relishes gambling (especially poker), loves fast cars, American football, jazz—and he's a physical-fitness nut. Her Highness is one of the Ten Best Dressed Women on every list, has a passion for jewelry, adores animals (her husband's hunting is one of the few loose ends in their otherwise tight-knit relationship), loves Italian opera, grows orchids, and enjoys all kinds of ballroom dancing. Both are nourished by publicity, love to meet people, revel in nightlife and always sleep until nearly noon.

In your planning, select and name five cities for their itinerary, and give full details of their movements in each. (Invent names of hotels, social events, people etc.) Suggest best time of year for this visit; give sightseeing destinations; nature, location and types of guests at official public functions (concerts, charity balls, etc.; you have the privilege of designing each one of these events); create a basic local volunteer committee organization that can be applied to each stop; and account for all other details that come up as you plan this extremely important, very demanding sequential event.

You must have $2 million total to work with, $1 million from state department funds. It's up to you to suggest ways for the local visit "committees" to raise the other $1 million to pay the bill.

You won't have any resistance to their visit from official metro units, but you've been strongly warned to expect taxpayer opposition, including noisy demonstrations, because of the government's partial subsidy of this visit and because of widespread political opposition to the government of their homeland.

You've decided that the RFP response is the best way to lay out your plans. What is your response?

14. New-Product Serial Event

THEME: "Peeling the Imagination." How can you get across the point to everyone that you're after creative ways thematically to use this great new product? Use this or your own theme.

A large national food manufacturer is rolling out a wonderful new product, called "Peelers," a wholesome, truly tasty snack product made from sweetened dried apple bits. This new product just happens to be superb as a baking ingredient as well, giving it an especially high appeal to women in the 25-54 age span (whether they'll admit it or not), who will use them in cooking and to provide a natural snack for their families.

There are five markets crucial to the successful introduction of "Peelers:" Chicago, San Francisco, Atlanta, Los Angeles and San Antonio. Its manufacturer believes if their target group will just taste this new product—and bake with it—they'll be sold for life.

That company has asked you to design a "serial event" concept that will play well, in sequence, in these five markets, by getting women to taste and bake with this wonderful new product.

For years, the company producing Peelers has had a strong charitable tie with Hope for the Homeless, a national organization to which the company has contributed millions of dollars over the years. With this project, the firm will make contributions again, an amount based on the number of public participants attracted to your promotion (so many dollars per participant). And in appreciation, Hope for the Homeless' volunteer support group members have offered to donate their time and efforts to help this promotion be a great success.

What "copyable" event can you design for sequential presentation in each of these cities, using the HH volunteers, and how do you prefer that it be implemented—by a traveling crew or by local hires supervised by traveling management?

Whatever you decide, how will you organize salaried and volunteer personnel in each city, providing each with a fully encompassing Position Description? Plan out every necessary detail, plus a fully-developed plan of efforts that must be completed even before the first city is visited. You have $2 million to spend, and not a penny more. (This is the second case study of the sixteen that does not require raising additional funding from sponsors.)

15. You're Kidding Yourself

THEME: See below; depends on several optional factors

Eventing for kids is one of the greatest challenges in this industry. You must be fast on your feet and several steps ahead to capture—and keep!—their attention . . . to really entertain them. But you are a brave (and highly creative) soul and have decided to open your own event design company, specializing in parties for children from four to twelve years of age.

You figure that you need a selection of at least sixteen themes for birthdays, Christmas, Halloween, along with other "manufactured" themes, to give clients a number of choices. What themes will you develop, bearing in mind the sophistication of today's youngsters?

To kick off and draw lots of attention to your new enterprise, you have decided to create a city-wide, kid-angled birthday party. You and other child-enterprise-related sponsors have tossed in a total of $50,000 for this big launching, but you'll need at least another $25,000 to make the splash you must have. (Remember your suppliers.)

You will want to be especially creative in getting media to cover this rather commercial event. Where and when will you have it? Who will you invite and why? Will your theme be based on the day or time of this huge party, or can you develop some other motif, possibly storybook and/or movie characters, one on what-do-you-want-to-be-when-you-grow-up idea, favorite games and pastimes, taking an imaginary trip somewhere, etc.

(This is the only option among the sixteen that is a single-day event, but it requires the same careful attention demanded by a much longer happening.) Use the RFP and response modes to detail your plans.

16. Music To Everybody's Ears

THEME: "Music: Everybody's Choice" or select one of your own.

Your chamber of commerce, in conjunction with several local musical organizations, art patrons and companies interested in promoting the arts and culture, have come up with $750,000 to fund a seven-day music festival. However, you know you'll need $250,000 more to make it really work, money you'll raise through additional sponsorships. How?

This amalgam knows that it has to please all musical tastes, but that's about all it knows, except for one other thing: they're aware that there are hundreds, perhaps thousands, of music festivals each year in this country. It would be wonderful if this could become the keystone event in your city annually. Therefore, they want this one to be different and better than all others. (Well, most of them, anyway.)

If it works this year, it could become an annual event in your city, perhaps with you in some high-paying position. In your RFP response to the chamber and me: Where and when will you stage this event? How will you make it different? What will be your entertainment mix that will be fresh and across-the-board appealing? What kinds of things will you create as support magnets—food, prize give-aways, sampling . . . what?

Very important: how will you make your local media material irresistible? Can you develop something so great that you'll get national media coverage?

ALTERNATIVE: REALITY CHECKS AS WAKE-UP CALLS

Although the above challenges are based on actual observances or perhaps possible cases here's one that will be based entirely on *your* very own living experiences:

A   If you are presently working in some capacity with a special event, set up two or three volunteer brainstorming sessions, either very soon or just after your event is held. Include all committee chairholders and let each bring one or two members.

Prepare your own RFP response just as if your event had not yet taken place. To start with, lead a discussion designed to reveal possible weaknesses, which can be corrected, and emphasize strengths on which to build further improvements. After the final session, draw up a summary of results and present them to your governing authority for serious consideration.

Fashion your response to a make-believe RFP, and fill it over the brim with fantastic new ideas and fresh improvements to old ones.

B. If you are a student or someone not presently directly involved in the functioning of an event, volunteer for one that especially interests you in your local area.

It can be a long- or short-term arrangement, perhaps with the promise of only a limited number of hours per week or month. And be up front; tell your new colleagues that you fully intend to carry your volunteer weight, but also want to study the event at the same time, your purpose being to eventually develop a *constructive* appraisal of its strong and weak points.

Your plan is to create your own RFP as a guideline for this study, even though your event may have been around a while. As you move concurrently through this book and your event study, prepare your RFP response as a class project or simply for your own (and perhaps your event's) benefit. Of course, you will be glad to provide them with your findings at the completion of your project.

And now, let's work with the information you will use in constructing your RFP responses.

Notes

[1]Two excellent adjuncts to these creativity exercises are *Think Out of the Box* (1995) and *Break Out of the Box* (1996); both from Career Press; $24.99 each, both authored by two experts in this field, my former Disney colleague, Mike Vance, and his associate, Diane Deacon.

[2]Since sponsorship is covered in far more detail in *SE:IO*, you might want to study that topic before developing a concept for this especially important need.

[3]Inclusions so designated (*) are taken from *Chase's Calendar of Events,* published annually by Contemporary Books, Inc., 2 Prudential Plaza, Suite #1200, Chicago, Illinois, 60601; Phone: (847) 679-5500; Fax: (847) 679-2494. Available in most large libraries. In place of the suggested workshop subjects herein, you may choose from others listed in Chase's Calendar. Be sure to have your own event listed in this excellent source; there is no listing charge.

Chapter Two

JOGGING AROUND ENTERTAINMENT

L et me make it really clear right here, before we go any further:

> **SPECIAL EVENTS ARE ENTERTAINMENT!**

That means showbiz, folks, whether we're talking festivals, competitions, fairs, even political conventions (in their own way)—every assemblage we think of as special events. And until everyone in the industry knows that, understands that and *practices that*, it's an industry that's not going to reach its enormous potential. There are still far too many eventers who don't.

Making *every* event, large or small, really entertaining should be our foremost goal, one that won't be any easier to achieve in the coming century. Why? Because of our competition.

Most of the world is already drenched in mega-powered, spectacular, technologically superior, and for the most part, supremely satisfying entertainment. At the turn of a TV dial or the slide of a few bucks into the box office slot, we can exchange often under-whelming what-is for overwhelming what-might-be—multi-million-dollar opening and closing ceremonies of international sporting events, halftime extravaganzas that bowl us over, dazzling special effects that recreate dinosaurs and de-create whole cities, fabulous production numbers that give life to otherwise dead awards ceremonies, splendid coronations, lavish royal weddings that lead us to juicy divorce scandals—and so on.

You can bet that worldwide entertainment is going to increase in opportunity numbers and in volume of excellence from the very outset of Century 21. Special events are their own species. In our own distinctive formats, our own unique nature, we can compete entirely successfully with all other forms of entertainment.

If we'll just rise up to several challenges.

One of the most important: stop fooling ourselves with numbers.

THE NUMBERS GAME

I should be used to it by now, but I'm not. I'm still get surprised by the estimated counts of event attendance calculated by calculating producers or law enforcement officials. If all their estimations were fact, Planet Earth would now glow red from the body heat of its twenty billion inhabitants (actual present count: five billion-plus). Perhaps—*perhaps!*— one in fifty is acceptably accurate with estimations; maybe one in a thousand underestimates attendance.

Overestimation feeds on its own inflation; producers and law enforcement officers had better show a constant attendance increase of, say, 2% or 3% or 5% or 7% with each edition, or they might have trouble proving their worth, keeping their jobs or justifying the very events themselves.

Eventers often point with pride to these swollen numbers, offering them as proof that they are, in fact, providing quality entertainment for visitors. "If we weren't, they'd stay away."

Wrong! Live by perception, die by deception.

Thanks to an expected growth in generous sponsorships, more and more events will be admissionless, or very low cost, in the coming century. A blessing and a challenge. Face it: many people (more than you may think) will always come out for *anything*, especially if it's free. Be it good or bad.

SYMPATHY FOR SYMPHONY

An unfortunate but all too typical example: a summer symphony concert. Every year a truly excellent symphony orchestra presents free concerts in three or four suburban satellites of its home city. Average attendance: between 12,000 and 15,000. Average number of avid enjoyers: I'll be generous, 2,000. By far, the majority are engaged in anything but listening—conversations, beer drinking, eating, trying to unbore bored kids (of whom there are thousands), napping—anything but *really* listening to and being *truly* entertained by this very excellent orchestra.

Attention levels increase a bit, but only temporarily, with some selections from Broadway shows or special-effects movies. About the only time close to full focus is captured comes at the program finale, traditionally "The Stars and Stripes Forever." With this Sousa cliché, even the rawest musical philistine is able to clap time with the march beat.

One problem is that every year, the orchestra brass (management, not the horns) decides that these summer concerts are excellent opportunities to promote music appreciation, so they throw in an obscure Mozart work, an even more obscure Vivaldi selection or a totally obscure Scarlotti number. Audience attention cuts out at about the third measure, if it even gets past the announced turnoff name of each piece. Motets, minuets, preludes, arias are deadly when performed outdoors in summer, except in cases where dedicated classical music lovers are the target audience.

Some contend that those concerts are among the most successful events in that metro area. Again, they use attendance figures (in this case, probably pretty close to factual count) to prove that point. I consider it successful only as proof of my contention that surprisingly large numbers of people will come out for a free anything, whether it's entertaining (to them) or not.

I have also seen countless parades that attracted many thousands of spectators, even though those processions were virtually identical to their previous ten, twenty or more editions. Using the axiom, "watch your audience, not the show" to meter performance acceptance, I paid close attention, finding that most spectators are far more interested in each other and food vendors than in the parade "entertainment." There is no argument, however; there were lots of people lining the route.

But is that what we in the events industry really want? People coming because it's free or there just isn't anything else to do or we offer convenient timing and location? I don't think so. I hope not. We should be magnetizing crowds because they *want* to be at our events, because those happenings are productions of quality, because they skew perfectly to their audiences or spectators.

SPECIES VS. SPECIES

You must be equally concerned about those who are *not* in attendance at your events. Why did they stay away? Can it be that your event has the same entertainment appeal as earwax removal? Does the entertainment package run the impact gamut from ho to hum? Have the blue-faced Tweedle twins, Dum and Dee, who render Beethoven's Fifth by blowing across bowling-ball holes, been booked a bit too often, this being their seventh consecutive year?

This issue does not suggest that your happening must be a three-dimensional, walk-in version of those televised or movie miracles. Obviously that's a ridiculous thought; they're of another species. Apples vs. oranges.

On the other hand, the *quality* special event species has its own distinctive and particularly appealing attributes:

- For one, our species are generally "right there;" it has the home territory advantage by playing well to its own constituency, its own neighbors. After all, it has been specifically designed for its own kind of people.

- For another, it's a time-favorable destination for enjoyment seekers, a visitable experience that doesn't fade to credits after two hours.

- And still another, it's a place of personal involvement and *direct* interaction with other people. By nature, most humans are pretty gregarious; events and parks are the only entertainment offerings that come close to fulfilling that near-instinct.

- Finally, as already noted, events and theme parks are the last bastions of *family*-style entertainment, a mission we should carefully guard and relentlessly pursue.

For these reasons, people can and will get up from their well-potatoed couches, leave their homes, drive, park (maybe take a shuttle), tolerate the elements (within reason), go to your event and *do* something—if it's really good and well marketed. They will because:

They're *involved.*

They're *part* of the goings-on.

They can interact.

They will be entertained,

And *not* because it's free, but because it's g-o-o-d.

Given a really appealing menu of demographically-based entertainment (music and non-), those positives tilt the playing field with big-time stuff from TV and movies several degrees in your favor.

When you offer them plenty to see, do and enjoy you'll also come closer to your don't-I-wish attendance estimates. Further, the more magnetism your event has, the far easier job its people have in selling those all-important sponsorships.

Which begins a remarkable round robin: more sponsorships almost always mean improved events, which sell more sponsorships, which means improved events . . . and so on.

IT'S ALL A MATTER OF IQ

Here are two suggestions that might help improve your IQ (interest quotient, in this case):

1. Know Your Audiences/Spectators

This is perhaps the oldest and wisest admonition in entertainment (along with "always leave 'em wanting more"). If you don't have a very thorough knowledge of the makeup of each group you're trying to please, the chances are better than good that you won't please them all that well.

If you're in a first-year operation, you should be as aware as older functions of the makeup of the audiences or spectators for whom your event is intended. If you are not, you shouldn't even be having it.

2. Know Your Audience/Spectator Preferences

Of course, not every member of every age group enjoys the very same kind of entertainment. There are rock-loving, gray-topped seniors and classical-loving, any-kind-of-topped teens. But not many of either. **Don't expect success when you play to the exceptions.**

Unfortunately, a surprising number of eventers still book talent to satisfy *their own tastes,* rather than those of their audiences or spectators. Sometimes that may happen because program management isn't always sure what those likes are. Try on these broad guidelines to make a match of multitudes with music:

Audience	Rap, Alter- native	Top 40	Album Rock	Adult Contem- porary	Easy Listen- ing	Oldies (1955- Now)	Big Band Nostalgia	Soft Adult Cont.	Country
GENERALLY PREFERRED MUSICAL ENTERTAINMENT									
Teens	✓	✓							✓
20s-30s	✓	✓	✓						✓
30s-40s				✓	✓				✓
40s-50s				✓	✓	✓		✓	✓
Seniors					✓	✓	✓	✓	✓

MUSICAL NOTES

- "Country" has a wide range of formats—classic, cross-over, western, folk and ethnic–which accounts for the grid-spanning interest indicated above.

- Obviously, music favoring narrower interests is a program option—*when it is clearly marketed as such.* This includes jazz, rhythm & blues, soul, gospel, the classics, music for young children, marches/patriotic and ethnic.

- Families respond especially well to musical variety shows, with something virtually for everyone, *but only in the middle grades above.* Leave out rap/hard rock and do limit country to the mid-taste area.

3.   Same Care in Programming All Other Entertainment

Perhaps these suggestions might help:

- Good storytellers are becoming bigger and bigger hits . . . and not only with the young. There are yarn-weavers who are highly accomplished in telling attention-grabbing adult stories (not *that* kind!).

- Stand-up comics continue to be popular. Of course, be sure their routines match the expectations of your audiences through auditions, reputation or pre-hire interviews. Some can get a bit gamy for an all-age crowd.

- Street performers—clowns, magicians, minstrels, jugglers, storybook characters—often add welcome entertainment punctuation to events. Mixing and mingling with crowds, as well as stage appearances, can make them valuable additions to your overall program mix. Although some worldly adults will disavow such, by and large, these entertainers are just as welcome by "mature" crowds as by younger ones. To make a greater impact, use your imagination; present them in some different, pleasantly unexpected manner.*

• Costumed mascots representing corporations, sports teams, etc. are often available at little or no cost and can brighten up your event. Check first, however, that there are no mascots representing competitors of your event sponsors—or get those sponsors to okay them before issuing invitations.

• [3]Arts-and-crafts has become such a popular "entertainment theme" of sorts that the market is glutted. Many thousand A&Cs are presented throughout the year in all major markets and too many minor ones. Don't succumb to the all-too-seductive lure of cookie-cutting by including this easy-to-do theme in your plans, if there are already A&Cs nearby. Or even if there aren't. Be creative! You just might come up with a really original, hot idea.

• If your event is of the type where this strategy would work well, put together your own entertainment groups. It's not as tough as it sounds, and these can be very attractive to sponsors. Some suggestions:

— **Ask a prominent church or educational choir director to recruit singers for a choral group.** And if local resources so indicate, think big. Suggest a group of 200-300, to become the Event Choral Society. Selection is done by audition tapes, in-person tryouts or established reputation for excellence.

— **Do the same with a local band and/or orchestra director, forming your own Event Concert Orchestra or Band.** He/she could also pull together the Event Alumni Marching Band, composed of more "now-mature" players who once performed as high school and/or college musicians. Do audition this group; they may have been away from their instruments a tad too long.

— **And once more, do the same with a highly qualified line-dance/cheerleader artist, bringing together your own Event Pep Squad.** They can be featured as "ambassadors" in pre-event promotional appearances, as well as serving as exciting event stage warm-up entertainers.

— **Kids and animals, *when used sparingly and properly,* can be a big success in your entertainment lineup.** It's my firm opinion that junior royalty and child amateur programs do *not* fall in the "sparingly and properly" category. Immediate families are about the only ones "entertained" by these weary, post-tiresome clichés. Mercifully, there is just a spark of indication that they're beginning to go out of style; let us do everything possible to encourage this infant movement. Then what do I have in mind as replacements? Try these or variations of them, if your event is appropriate, but remember the brick! Distinguish them from their usual formats with themes, decorations, perhaps venues, etc.

— **Paws, claws and jaws, a kids' pet parade and show**. Old hat? You bet, but for some mystical reason, they usually work very well, especially with media—particularly when staged in fresh, creative ways. Prizes here go to the ugliest, cutest, youngest, most unusual, etc. (This concept is about as far removed from those uppity, haughty purebred dog and pony shows put on by the horsy set as it can be.)

— **Stage one of those uppity, haughty purebred dog and pony shows put on by the horsy set, which are about as far removed from the above as possible**. Work with local breeders, horse farms, animal training clubs, groomers, etc., to see if their annual or a special show can be worked into your event. If your happening is established and well attended, it can be a big thrust in public interest for these animal production numbers, both in terms of media, attendance and image.

— **Surefire high entertainment ratings always go to those remarkable demonstrations by K9 law enforcement units** and by dogs assisting those persons with sight, hearing or other physical challenges. Check local animal groups, law enforcers and support groups; you may find a super no- or low-cost show.

* There are surprising numbers of other no- or low-cost options available for event inclusion, even in smaller towns. Generating great interest are model railroad setups (some of which are works of art), model car and airplane collections and demonstrations, sports card displays (which can move quickly into attendance-building trading sessions, as can pin exchanges), display or trading of other collectables (comic books, for example), museum-promoting loan-outs, used-book sales, law enforcement/fire/rescue equipment demonstrations and many others.

* Ask local florists, nurseries and landscape architects to come together to *voluntarily* organize your own Event Flower and Garden Show—and while they're at it, ask them to decorate your site with mostly borrowed, reclaimable plants, along with beds, planters and pots of flowers.

* If your event is of the type where this is appropriate, work with professionals, asking them to serve as volunteers to create your own on- or off-site:

golf tournament	**horseshoe games**
tennis tournament	**softball tournament**
racquetball tournament	**volleyball tournament**
swim meet	**archery competition**
diving competition	**foot races**
horse, bicycle and/or auto race(s)	**bowling**

Incidentally, each of these is especially ripe for title sponsorship and reasonable registration fees, which means they can become profit centers for your event.

4. Don't Waste Your Entertainment and Other Dollars on Pre-Event Media Happenings.

Advocates contend that these "promotions" begin to focus attention on the event. But I contend that you'll spend bucks for programming only a comparatively few people are likely to attend. They're supposed to build up public interest, primarily through media coverage. If your publicists are the dynamos you need, they'll be building public interest well ahead of Day One by implementing a strong strategy of quality, fresh-idea material with your media. Use every dollar, including those labeled "entertainment," for your event itself. Far more powerful is a special media and VIP event tour the day before or the morning of Day One. (See Chapter 4)

5. Don't Clone Last Year's Entertainment Lineup

Let me say it again: *Don't make your production an annual reproduction.* This problem very often starts with the selection of entertainment. Eventers find a collection of performers, know where to find them, know what they cost, and feel they can't do any harm with a Return Engagement/Return Engagement I/Return Engagement II/Return Engagement III/Return Engagement Ad Infinitum. Bad idea.

Of course, if you have one or more performers who are very obvious favorites with your kind of people, you'll be expected to bring them back. But surround your stables with the air-fresheners of new offerings. Who knows? New ones may become favorites, too.

6. Self-Competition: How Many Stages?

Events often dilute effectiveness of their entertainment fare in the mistaken belief that attendance numbers always directly parallel an event's entertainment quantity. They don't. But change the last "quantity" to "quality," and I'll agree entirely.

There is one often frequently denied truism in the event industry: the fewer choices event-goers have to make, the better they like it. Most guests will never admit it, but they *enjoy being benevolently controlled.* Subtly, of course. One highly successful producer of a huge festival summed it up very well when he said that the typical event-goer "would be pretty darned happy if he/she could just sit in one place and have good food, drink and entertainment brought to him/her."

Relegating each particular style of music and/or classification of performance to its own stage or area can produce an overall better balanced entertainment program that makes choices easier.

A workable festival might be:

STAGE ONE— (highest audience capacity)—spectacles, headliners and biggie general crowd-pleasing offerings;

STAGE TWO—non-musical acts (caution: only certain comedy and magic routines work well outdoors; pre-check with potential performers);

STAGE THREE—preteen programs alternating with those for young children;

STAGE FOUR—country rotating with specialties—ethnic, jazz, r&b, etc.

STAGE FIVE—top pop for teens and young adults.

For smaller festivals with fewer stages, set aside appropriate day parts for each of these divisions—morning for kids and pets and non-musical presentations; afternoon for families; early evening—spectacles and big shows; late evening—older teens and younger adults.

If your event is directed to a narrower audience, you may have the same type of entertainment offered on two or three stages, but keep smaller numbers of stages busy with good presentations, rather than filling a larger number with make-do fillers. When dealing with anything related to special events, where there's a choice of quality vs. quantity, *always take the former.* This is especially true of entertainment.

7. Positioning Your Open-Air Stages is Crucial

I cannot count the times I have visited events with stages angled exactly wrongly. It's as if they've hired mathematicians, astronomers and rocket scientists to place those stages precisely where they shouldn't be. Here are some important factors—

— *First consideration:* is each platform facing an area that will easily and comfortably accommodate the expected audience size? If not, you may have to move or offer duplicate shows with ticket control, even if tickets are free.

— *Really important:* where will the sun be during performances? *It should be shining into the stage from behind audience heads.* If the stage is to be used all day during warm months, if at all possible, position it to face south, with spectators looking north. There still might be an audience-sun problem during early morning and late afternoon hours, but that would be the minimum bright-in-the-eye inconvenience inflicted on your audiences/spectators.

8. Fireworks and/or Laser Shows

These favorites can have gigantic and memorable impacts on spectators—again, *if* they're effectively presented.

Fireworks are long-established event favorites—Big Time! Just don't make pyrotechnic shows too lengthy; they're far more electrifying if big clusters of shootings are compacted into fifteen or twenty minutes, rather than being dribbled out with a shot or two every few minutes during an hour-long presentation.

Be even more careful with lasers. They can be expensive, but extra compelling if used artfully in fast-paced groupings. Unless created by big-time experts, a one-laser-beam show is about as "special" or "grand" as a single string of spaghetti at an Italian dinner.

9. Watch the Audience or Spectators—*NOT* THE SHOW

I alluded to this practice earlier, but it bears repeating with elucidation. Once you've got a show to the point of public presentation, *don't check out the show* to see how it's going over, *watch the people in front of it.*

No matter what the stage action may be, if this show is not for this crowd, for any reason, their actions will speak a lot louder than whatever applause they may offer out of politeness. Shuffling in seats; whispering or talking; yawns; reading something; nail-cleaning, -filing or -biting—all are the only "reviews" you need to let you know that you have a problem.

10. *QUALITY* is the Big Difference Between *TRADITION* and *REPETITION*.

Those of you fortunate enough to have seen the changing of the guard at Buckingham Palace have been fortunate enough to see *quality*. Ditto for torch-lighting ceremonies, certain very special parades, Presidential oath-taking rites, etc. No matter how often you see these happenings, they're as exciting and fresh as they were the first time you enjoyed them. That's because of an inherent, hard-to-define characteristic, called *quality*.

Conversely, yawn-spawners are often staged over and over again, wrongly in the name of tradition. Truth be known, they're repetitions and nothing more. Do a close "physical check-up" on your event. Are you guilty of repetition instead of real tradition? Are you doing something repeatedly ("We've done it for years, why stop now?") because it's easy to do, regardless of its low attention magnetism and perhaps obvious lack of quality?

Don't rely on personal verbal responses from members of your audiences/spectators, especially if your event has free admission and/or is held to benefit a cause. Only a few will say anything negative; the remainder won't bother or are too considerate or embarrassed to be honest with you.

Try new ideas in place of old ones until that elusive ingredient, quality, makes itself known.

Hear me out as I compare quality to pornography; you may not always be able to describe it, but you recognize it when you see it.

FOOD FOR THOUGHT AS ENTERTAINMENT

You don't consider food to be entertainment? Try having any kind of party of almost any size without offering food. People rarely eat at events because they're hungry; they do so because they enjoy it. It's a big part of special events. To me, that's entertainment.

Generally, American happenings do very well in the food department. That's because our countrymen, largely descending from pioneer stock where food was more important than just about anything else, still put high value on the quality of vittles. To perpetuate a viable event, savvy eventers, therefore, frequently check the quality of their edibles.

Doing something special with food can add particularly pleasant, unexpected embellishments to your more conventional entertainment lineup. Examples:

— Cooking demonstrations are great pleasers. Crowds love these, especially when samples are distributed. Another plus: they add marvelous fragrances that appeal strongly to olfactory senses.

— Cooking competitions.[2] These have been regular fare at fairs, in some cases, for as long as a hundred years. Almost any event theme, however, lends itself to such entertainment.

— For sporting and athletic events, food tournaments might pivot on low or no fat, calories, cholesterol, sodium, etc., healthful, energy-giving dishes that are actually *tasty*.

— For arts and crafts doings, competitors see who can produce the most tantalizing, picturesque, unusual food still lifes.

— For animal themes, try to come up with interesting new versions of hot dogs, hush-puppies, mousse, and horseradish uses, maybe bird's nest soup, as well as human food featuring animal decorations, and animal food made to look like human favorites—ice cream sundaes, carrot cake, baked Alaska, cherries jubilee, Brie, etc., creatively made from canned or dry pet food.

— Food stylist demonstrations are always favorites. Not how to cook, but how to make food *look* its very best. That is the mission of food stylists. Their how-to presentations can captivate audiences, especially when offering really easy-to-do suggestions requiring little or no artistic qualifications or particularly costly equipment. Again, stylists can direct their demonstrations to the specie of your event—community/family , sports/athletic, animal, religious, waterways, patriotic, December and other holidays, music, arts and crafts, etc.

FOOD SPECIALTY ADVANTAGES

Some festivals rely entirely on food themes as their very reasons for being—beans, garlic, nuts (wal and pea); cereals, berries (rasp, blue and straw), avocados, chili, seafood, to name just a few. Food-oriented though your event may not be, you can (and should) try to develop a specialty that, when its name is even mentioned, immediately brings to mind your event.

Some possibilities: mold-pressed ice cream or candy in the shape of a cotton boll; pine cone; nuts (wal and pea); berries (rasp and straw); balls (base, foot, soccer, volley, basket, tennis, golf, bowling and ping-pong); clock; event or sponsor logo; landmark building, bridge or structure; animal heads; musical instruments; a concoction of nuts and berries (wal, pea, straw, blue and rasp) and so on.

Incidentally, a specialty food can become an instrument of marketing. Each year, the first one produced is presented ceremoniously to some worthy recipient—with the media present, of course. Its production and use can make good feature material, as well. And naturally, when the 10,000[th], 50,000[th], 100,000[th], etc. is sold, it becomes a media ceremony.

Well, so much for food for thought . . . and thoughts for food.

Notes

[1] Even such an established format as that for parades can be given a creative overhaul. At the 1994 (then named) International Festival Association convention, I introduced the concept I call PARADE REST. It lets spectators do the moving while the parade itself remains in a fixed position. This approach is useful for so many newer suburbs not having "downtown" thoroughfares suited to the standard parade format. It can also work well on many special event sites.

[2] An important caution: before you schedule food competitions be sure to check with your local jurisdictional controller of public food service to determine requirements, necessary licenses and ordinances. And of course, abide by these assiduously. Usually this is a health or public safety agency.

[3] I must admit to a somewhat prejudiced attitude toward the A&C category. There are so many; a few good ones, true, but huge numbers of really bad ones, at least in my opinion. I try to judge only the overall effect of the shows I visit, and to take into account what attendees say about them. But I'm FAR from an arts/crafts connoisseur; I can never decide whether I'm judging them with an artless heart or whether they're looking back at me as heartless art.

Chapter Three

LOOKING GOOD - BEING GOOD[1]

When you know you look good, you just naturally feel better about yourself. And that goes for events, too. They actually feel "up" when they *know* they have great eye appeal. There is a direct correlation between appearance and overall quality of their other components—entertainment, games, competitions, social interplay, organizational integrity . . . whatever.

And just how do you dress up an event to give it high eye appeal? One obvious answer is, of course, with decorations. But to look at too many of our events, you would think that a large number of people in our industry either don't know the value of decorations or don't think that value is weighty enough to warrant special attention – and enough bucks. Others simply don't know how to decorate well or it just didn't occur to anyone to take these enhancements into account.

It is my firm belief that decoration planning and funding should be right up there pretty close to the highest operational and budgetary priorities of every event, whether it's a church social or a festival with a million or more people-visits.

There's no doubt; deft decorating puts an event's best face forward.

THE EYES HAVE IT

People arriving know they're at a special occasion the moment they see well deployed decorations. (You know, first impression and all that.) And this special feeling stays with them as they're brought repeatedly into contact with decorations throughout an event's run, whether it's a few hours, several days or maybe even a couple of weeks.

Decorations also serve other important needs. They:

— can quickly and firmly fix a theme (see p. 43*ff*) and provide an immediate visual *raison d'être* for the event;

— convert an otherwise drab, dreary or generally unattractive venue into a happier, more inviting setting;

— visually reduce the size of an area too large for the expected number of celebrants, to conceal embarrassing empty seats or bare spaces. If a larger group shows, simply reposition the decorations;

— add substantially to and emphasize strongly the dramatic, ceremonial, comedic, achievement recognition or other primary event formats and contents;

— and they can be a source of sometimes significant revenue as a high visibility sponsorship opportunity.[2]

COST? EFFECTIVE?

Even if it were possible, it would be a disservice to recommend an across-the-board, all-event budgetary percentage for decorations, but it should be right up there with food, entertainment, communications, marketing, transportation, etc. Decorations are *very* important.

Too many event administrators do not exercise their imagination muscles when considering these site enhancements. Creativity can produce fresh, delightful, fully effective decorations at surprisingly reasonable costs. Suggestions:

- **Look for materials that are inexpensive and buy them in quantities from the same vendor.**

  One large, indoor event effectively used scores of yards of veil-like netting in three pastel shades, originally priced at twenty-nine cents a yard but reduced ten percent through a volume purchase. Volunteers puffed it, clumped it, draped it and swathed with it, ending up with a remarkably effective decorative panorama. Incidentally, by careful removal and storage, they were able to return that material to use more than once.

- **Use materials that are not usually thought of for your particular need.**

  Everyone has seen first-hand or on television the plastic "caution—do not cross" yellow plastic tape used by law enforcers to isolate crime scenes.

  This material is comparatively inexpensive, and special wording—event name or its subdivisions ("Fun Zone," "Art Walk," etc.)—can be ordered at little extra cost. It is also easy to attach, it's durable as well as weather resistant, and it can be used more than once with careful dismantling and storage.

  This tape can be draped or hung in continuous, same-or-variable-length strips for such purposes as stage backdrops, covering unsightly surfaces or separating booths in a trade-show-like grid; wrapped around columns, poles and tree trunks; swung hammock-like to create false ceilings or shade from a searing sun; tagged in long strips to the top of high poles to wave in the breeze as streamers; and braided for attachment to stanchions for crowd control.

  Other items available in large numbers, sizes or lengths, which can be forced to become visually and cost effective decorations are:

  — **Fish netting.** It can be spray-painted or dyed—and not necessarily used only with nautical themes.

  — **Cheese cloth, gauze or similar inexpensive materials.** With a "fabric paint" or dye application, it can be used in a number of imaginative ways.

— **Continuous sheets of computer track paper**. Imprint it with messages and/or stripe it with poster paints, and three- to six-foot-long sections of its perforated edges make great hanging confetti after applications of various colors of poster or similar paint. For any porous material or surface, always test paints to be sure you'll get the results you want.

— **Holiday garland.** Although definitely a specific decoration, it need not make appearances only during December every year. Yards of not-only-Christmas colors—silver, gold, white, purple, blue— can be picked up at bargain prices in late December. Worked together artfully, they become highly effective decorations that won't necessarily betray their seasonal origins.

— **Plants in portable planters.** These delights are among the most desirable enhancements. Potted shrubs can break up severe tent or structural lines, or create a broad pedestrian boulevard. Even small trees can take some of the edge off terrifically hot days, just by "being there." Try borrowing these from local nurseries or florists. If that doesn't work, as suggested later, attempt to line up those firms, along with landscape architects, garden clubs, etc., as in-kind sponsors, that "in-kind" being the loan or donation of things that are growing.

— **Cardboard and/or wooden boxes and crates**. If they're in structurally sound condition, these otherwise ugly ducklings can be transformed into beautiful swans with spray paint, perhaps a drape or outline of fringe or lace; a patina of carefully applied bright paper or cloth material; a veneer of richly-grained, nicely finished plywood or Formica®, etc. When various shapes or sizes are clustered, they can have high-powered appeal without ever revealing their dermal secrets. Pierced by short flag or banner poles, directional sign posts and so on, they become attractive, practical anchors. Perfectly cubed containers can become dramatic giant A-B-C building blocks keynoting a children's area or attraction.

— **Using bales of hay** is an old standby. Problem is, most events let them be just bales of hay. Yards of vinyl or lower-cost material can immediately dress them up, tie them directly to your color scheme or theme, and make them add to, rather than detract from, your event. Covered bales can also make great "park benches," flankers for roads and walkways, safety buffers for kid contain-ment and moderate protection from minor hazards. Undecorated, they're okay for a hoedown theme, but that's about all.

— **Scrap or unused plywood, drywall sheets or planks.** Again, these resurrected items, when spruced up, can become comely money-savers, which can be impressed into a number of event services. Quick but thorough spray painting (usually two to three coats, at least) can convert these uninspired slob-slabs into colorful rectangles for fencing, stage backdrops, and partitions separat-ing event divisions. One event recently painted scrap plywood sections stark white and loaned celebrants wide felt markers in different colors to scribble their own messages (an attendant as-sured that all graffiti were socially acceptable), thus "personalizing" the event. It was called "The Great Sign-Up Wall," and it became the most photographed single backdrop at that large event.

— **Sonotubes®**. Again, these items are not really decorations at all; they're durable forms for casting concrete cylinders. Suggested primarily for events with expansive vistas, Sonotubes make excel-lent, very dramatic, powerful decorations. They come in a variety of diameter spans (from eight-inch. to thirty-six-inch.) and in twelve-foot lengths. Prices (subject to change, of course) vary from area to area, averaging between $2.30 and $4.20 a linear foot. But it doesn't take many of these stand-on-end grouped pillars, which can be painted, wrapped, glittered, etc., to make a lasting memory. And fortunately, they can be repeatedly redecorated for several years of fresh-looking use. Check with local contractors, who may donate any "left-overs" or join you as an in-kind sponsor to contribute these versatile, highly durable forms.[3]

■   **Carefully plan decoration placement.**

This may seem an unnecessary suggestion, but again, too many eventers don't follow it. Just to be sure, check these placement suggestions:

—   Recruit a successful interior designer, decorator or architect to serve as executive volunteer head of your Decorations Committee (see Chapter 6) and/or be named an in-kind sponsor as a contributor of time, talent and materials. This strategy can go a long way in providing your event with a professional look through a greater impact from decorative accessories.

—   For further visual boldness, cluster "bouquets" of decorations rather than putting a piece here, one or two over there, etc. Clustering can make the most of an anemic decorations budget. But even with a robust one, cluster anyway.

—   Carefully check your event's pedestrian and vehicular traffic patterns, then group decorations at points of greatest use – where more eyes are bound to enjoy them.

—   Let your enhancements play a major marquee role for your event. As part of your decorations, bannering and signage plans, focus significant attention on your main and secondary entrances, where decorations can attract and entice impulse drop-ins, as well as direct planned visitors to the right location(s).

—   Require a frequent decorations check throughout the run of your event, to be certain they look their very best at all times and that you continue to be satisfied with their placement. Be sure that you have allowed some reserve decorations to fill in when damage, theft, fading, etc., afflict any of the "first run" items.

—   Speaking of theft, stolen decorations are one of the most common event problems. Whenever possible, display your decorations as high as is reasonable and in a difficult-to-access location. Well-lighted areas with lots of foot or wheeled traffic are also desirable—and they also provide maximum enjoyment of those enhancements.

HOW MANY REPS?

It depends on the nature of your decorations as to how many encores you should plan for a given wardrobe of accessories.

Particularly rich, imaginative, really outstanding decorations are proud and willing victims of their own excellence in terms of their resurrectablity. Their initial impact is so great that it wears down very quickly, causing them to slip into the ho-hum, been-there, seen-that mode, often as fast as by second usage—and certainly by the third.

But do not let this once-or-twice-over-lightly cycle daunt your objective of creating decoration spectaculars. Your event could actually become known for its always-exciting looks from year to year, thanks to fresh, especially appealing, *creative* decorations.

When embellishments are so imbedded in our psyche that their uses are set for us, you have no choice; you may be *required* to use them. Those icons can be used over and over again with our visual blessings—*providing imagination places them in different arrangements and locations from use to use.*

Examples are red, white, and blue bunting, the flag and other American symbols, which are expected to be used on patriotic occasions. Certainly a July 4th festival could hardly qualify as such if it did not use these basics. However, *creativity* is especially important in such uses, in terms of placement, clustering and other interesting arrangements that should change from one edition to another.

Among decorations that can be used repeatedly—again, hopefully with new formats and fresh applications each time—are those for Christmas, Hanukkah, New Year's, Valentine's Day, St. Patrick's Day, Easter, Purim, Halloween and Thanksgiving. There may be others for such purposes as religious rites, sports, celebrations of other nations' historical events, a unique local observance, etc.

Words of caution, however: early on, very carefully inspect decorations to be reused for fading, fraying, rips, and permanent soilage. If components can't be made entirely presentable, they are evil and must be destroyed. Get new ones.

TELL 'EM WHERE TO GO

Strongly related to decorations, signage is very frequently a neglected element in too many events. Oh, of course, most are understandably quick to display sponsor banners, and rightfully so. But what about equally important directional, assistance and visitor-comfort signs?

When planning a new or encore event, put yourself in the place of a stranger/first-time visitor. It will be obvious to you that you *must* clearly indicate the following by on-site signage *and/or* easy-to-follow, *free* maps in generous supply:

— **exact locations of restrooms and potable water stations**.

— **where and how trash must be deposited**. This is especially necessary when recycling dictates separation of various trash materials— paper, glass, plastic, etc.

— **locations and programming times** within your event. Let everyone know when and where special performances will take place; locations and visiting times of any important short-term exhibits; starting/ending points, routes and timing of parades, etc.

— **directions to parking areas**. Each lot should be given an easy-to-remember name on well-displayed signs. Be sure to indicate reserved parking spaces for volunteers; on-duty governmental personnel from health departments, law enforcement units, public safety services and the like; event staff; performers; sponsors and handicapped

— **strict restrictions**: no smoking, no alcohol, etc. Keep these to a minimum; too many rules are offensive and cloud up what should be a clearly festive atmosphere. Make sign messages "friendly but firm," perhaps using cartoon-like characters on signs to dull their cutting, preachy effect. Do post absolutely required restrictions with enough frequency that no person need be embarrassed by being personally reminded of them by a security rep.

- **Especially clear directions to first-aid and other medical services.**

- And **facilities** for handling—

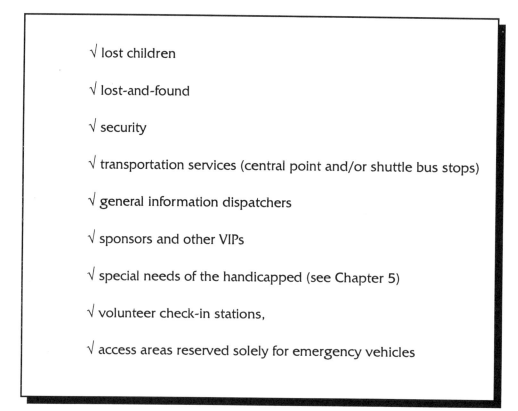

√ lost children

√ lost-and-found

√ security

√ transportation services (central point and/or shuttle bus stops)

√ general information dispatchers

√ sponsors and other VIPs

√ special needs of the handicapped (see Chapter 5)

√ volunteer check-in stations,

√ access areas reserved solely for emergency vehicles

MAKING SIGNS FIT

Nothing is more offensive to the eye nor can as quickly abolish polish than hand-printed, "homemade" signs, requiring tongue-between-teeth, tortured printing with a black felt marker on a new-shirt stiffener of gray cardboard. Not cool.

Good event planning takes into account signage needs, allowing plenty of time and funds to have them made by a quality sign shop. But do check around; you'll frequently find similar quality at dissimilar prices from shop to shop. Also, you might try to get that work done on an in-kind sponsorship basis.

However, if you do find need for unplanned signs, and must create them on the spot, use any one of the several sign-making systems available through most well-stocked art supply houses. Peel-off vinyl and stencil-format are the most popular and effective sign-making processes that can be used pretty effectively after a bit of practice. Again, check around; there can be a big difference in prices for very similar systems.

HAVING A HEALTHY COLOR

Selection and use of color for event decorations and signs can be dynamite. . . one way or another. Color can be positively powerful . . . or powerfully explosive. Here are some tips for effective color use:

- **Consider introducing a new basic color palette for your event, if your present one has been in use several years or if it was a bad choice to begin with.**

   This substitution can do cosmetic wonders for your event—IF you make the right choice. Suggestion: take your need to a highly respected decorator, architect or designer, asking their advice . . . without charging you, of course.

- **Remember: very bright, lively shades often appear to consume more space than softer hues.**

   If you are decorating a small, perhaps crowded space, reds, oranges, yellows, etc. might tend to make that space seem even smaller, perhaps more crowded or cluttered. Try pastels.

- **Take your colors from the Pantone® Matching System, which offers a 1000-color selector.**

   But borrow one; they're pricey, especially for a one- or two-time need. Color users, including especially printers, go by Pantone's® color codes, or "PMS" (sic!) numbers. Find your color codes and stick to 'em. If you select that beautiful shade of red, PMS #032, stay with it or within two or three shades of it—max!

   One of the greatest pitfalls of decorating is calling on a hodgepodge of mixed colors and shades; it's really tacky when your "reds" range in shades from sparrow's mouth pink to badly-bruised-apple reddish brown. Select two or three—four at the absolute most—really good, work-well-together colors, specifying their code numbers and staying with them. Be really cranky with anyone tampering with your established PMS color selection.

- **On signs, remember to use sufficiently contrasting colors to facilitate readership.**

   Often visitors merely glance at signs quickly or need that information at night or in heavy shadows. Also the fewer words, the better, so long as you don't lose intended meanings. A final word about color: be sure your signs are color-coordinated with your decorations palette.

TESTING YOUR SITE

Have you looked at—no, *really studied* —the current or potential site of your event? Every other thing may be in top condition, but if your site is bad, your event starts off muscle-bound. Here's an exercise appraisal guide to help you determine what changes, if any, your location may need:

- **Are you wedded to this particular site?**

   Your event may have outgrown its location or may never have lived up to its potential because of its site. Do you need more room, better vehicle and pedestrian accesses, prettier surroundings, a more appealing neighborhood, a locale in a politically and socially friendlier climate? Don't be afraid to make a move, but don't overdo it in frequency, either. Frequent site shifting can really confuse visitors.

- ## Do you suffer from the here-there-everywhere syndrome?

  Is your event needlessly cut up into pieces that are spread all over hell-and-gone? In nearly every case, when scattered shards of an event are pieced together on a single site and situated at the right point, attendance increases and sponsors are more abundant and generous. Visitors, who can park in one place for a full day's worth of offerings, rather than having to drive to and park at five or six locations, will. And sponsors, who can send their messages in the biggest format at only one or two places, rather than having to duplicate efforts at five or six locations, will.

- ## Is your site presentable at all times?

  Cleanliness is just about on an equal level with Godliness in terms of event-site presentation. It's a source of amazement at how many eventers can look but not see:

---

weeds that need zapping—or—garbage that needs wrapping

lawns that need mowing—or—torn things that need sowing

other things that need repair—or—others that need paint care

blank areas that need . . . something!—or—decorations that need bumping

bare spots that need reseeding—or—ugly areas that need concealing

walks that need swept—or—floors that aren't kept

windows that need cleaning—or—surfaces that need preening

metal that needs brightened—or—loose things that need tightened

noisy things that need qui-eting—or—junky things that just aren't exci-eting

---

- ## Does your scene have good scents?

Nose sores are just as devastating to events as eye sores. First and foremost, portable potties should be *very carefully* positioned (consider prevailing wind direction), but still easy to see when needed most urgently. And make sure they're serviced several times daily, along with all indoor rest rooms.

Food waste on a hot day can very quickly move from being obnoxious to being almost noxious. Tend to food areas repeatedly. Stop those odors before they start.

Meanwhile, make maximum use of fragrance givers – well prepared food being cooked or baked, generously placed flowers and fragrant trees, scented candles and oil lamps (triple-check for safety), cleaning supplies that do, in fact, *smell clean,* etc.

But be careful in your selection of air-fresheners for enclosures. Some are just plain sickening. Also, always be conscious that, in confined spaces, perfumed scent can cause enormous discomfort to those sensitive or allergic to fragrances.

THE HEARING TEST

We've considered the needs to look good and smell good, but there's still one more matter to consider: is your event in *sound* shape? Are you too near an airport, train tracks, well-trafficked harbor, industrial center or hyper-busy freeway? You may want to investigate the relocation option.

On-site, you must have totally reliable stage-sound and public address systems. Provide baffling and "aim" sound systems so that your activities don't fire volleys of high-decibel shots into otherwise quiet residential neighborhoods or business centers.

Further words about baffling. Sometimes tree groves, rolling terrain and solid building walls can help greatly. If you are not fortunate enough to have such permanent sound barriers, try to position your tents or fencing to absorb as many decibels as possible. Large canvas or vinyl paneling, suspended as decorations or signage between sturdy high polls is an option, but possibly a costly one. If you plan to occupy the same site(s) repeatedly, the investment might be worthwhile.

But use stage and/or speaker-system "aiming" as your primary line of defense against unneighborly sound intrusion. "Surround Sound" is great for your home entertainment center; it's not for event neighborhoods.

THINK THEMEING

There are two themeing levels: (1) overall, perennial ones and (2) those that change annually.

Examples of (1) are those already mentioned that annually celebrate food, using that food to set a pervasive theme. There are also air shows, jazz events, and of course, patriotic ones, such as those saluting July 4th.

Events in category (2) are usually generic in nature, but overlay a different theme patina from year to year, such as a city-wide family festival that might have a movie motif one year, a nautical theme the next and perhaps one on music the third.

Some eventers think negatively of themeing. They say it's too limiting. Truth is, their *imagination* is often the problem because it hasn't been given enough exercise.

Walt Disney indisputably proved the value of themeing when he created Disneyland with its Main Street U.S.A, Tomorrowland, Adventureland and Fantasyland themes, in the mid-1950s.

Each land's overall panorama down to its tiniest details adheres to the established motif – everything from live entertainment to trash receptacles. *There are no exceptions.* I'm not suggesting that special events, almost always operating with very limited funds, can hope to match that most remarkable permanent event called Disneyland and its larger Florida sibling. But they can try.

To theme an event *artfully and effectively* bestows on it the following:

— **COHESIVENESS.** Things look as if they belong together *because they do.* For eventers and visitors, there's that same satisfying feeling people get when they've assembled a whole jigsaw puzzle.

There's also a strong sense of togetherness, of visual strength, of planned solidity. It promotes a feeling of comfort and becomes a source of enjoyment . . . of lasting recollections. "Gosh, wasn't that well done," is a frequently heard tribute for the fair-of-face, themed events.

— **DISTINCTION.** Themes can declare and establish a favorable individuality to an event, actually very often becoming a substantial marketable asset – an irresistible sponsor inducement. Let's play a game:

QUESTION ONE: Quickly! What events do you think of first when you hear "flowered floats," "huge inflatable character balloons," "Mardi Gras," "biggest-time football," "biggest-time base-ball," "experimental aircraft," "world baseball play-offs for kids," etc.?

There was very little doubt about the single selections brought to top-of-mind instantly by each theme, was there?

QUESTION TWO: Now just as quickly: what do you think of immediately when you hear "family festival," "summer festival," "winter festival," "water (lakes, rivers, creeks, oceans, etc.) festival," "arts and crafts show," "marathon"? Notice how solid distinctions failed to materialize with these broadly categorized, very general labels.

Of course some answers to Question Two depend on where you live. If you're an east-coaster, you are likely to tie "marathon" to Boston or New York. But for those listed in Question One, there are few or no choices. "Because they're large," you say. They weren't always. They became big and popular because they had distinction and quality – and themeing played a major role in their successes.

I'm always sorrowfully amazed at how many times I've found scores (sometime hundreds) of dedicated volunteers donating hundreds of hours of really hard work, along with tons of talent, to happenings that reached only a smidgen of their potential. Now themeing, perpetual or rotational, won't solve all problems, of course, but it certainly stands a big chance of contributing to higher quality.

And I'm certainly including those annual events that set a theme each year and stick to it. Almost inevitably, they become quality standouts because of their creative, solidifying overlays.

— **EASE OF IMPLEMENTATION**. That's right. Pulling together a themed event is no more difficult than assembling an eclectic one. In some instances, it has actually helped implementation.

Very often, you can theme by giving different names to entertainment, pedestrian avenues, clustered tent areas, volunteers, etc. (see below). You'll see that it isn't at all difficult.

You know your event will need trash receptacles, banners, decorations, vehicles, volunteer t-shirts (nearly always), signs, etc. To theme, you either go after only those items that fit your theme, or you take those that don't *and change 'em.*

THEMEING IN ACTION

Let's take another journey into imagination, this time to help understand themeing more clearly.

You and I are now partners (co-executive directors, extravagantly paid) for a pretty well-established municipal "family-class" festival. We agree that it needs to be more fit, and we've decided to lay on a different theme every year as one refresher.

For our first try at themeing we've chosen a truly universal experience that ties in well with the arrival of the new century. Our theme:

TIME

We've already had an especially successful brainstorming session with our volunteers and several highly respected advisors. In that session we listed everything we could think of that deals in any way with time. Here's our *partial* list:

Clocks, alarm clocks, travel clocks, grandfather's clocks, cuckoo clocks, o'clock, 1-12 o'clock, Big Ben (it's really the chimes, not the clock, but anyway), watches, stopwatches, Mickey Mouse watches, sun dials, hourglasses, seconds, moments, instants, minutes, hours, weeks, months, January-December, days, years, decades, centuries, millennia, ages, epochs, eras, eternity, chronology, calendars,

Mornings, evenings, nights, dawn, dusk, seasons, winters, summers, falls, springs, sands of time, timing is everything, time flies, time heals all wounds, how fast time passes, an idea whose time has come, time of your life, waste of time, it's about time, period of time, what time is it?, do you have the time?, the time of day, point in time, to be on time, "Time on My Hands," "One Moment in Time,"

"As Time Goes By," "Time and Again," "Get Me to the Church on Time," be on time, late, punctual, Time Magazine, Bulova, Seiko, timetable, timeline, timeframe, lifetime, timely, tempo, morning glories, "four o'clock" flowers, minutemen, yesterday, today, tomorrow, time is money, only a matter of time, keep in time, killing time, short-timer,

Neither the time nor the place, one thing at a time, pass the time away, "Days of Our Lives," so little time, don't have the time right now, hard times, turn back time, time-honored, timeless, "Those Were the Days," good ol' times, "Dance the Whole Night Away," signs of the times, Christmas-time, out of time, time out, pastime, days/months/etc. on end, and on and on and on.

With this list in hand, here's what we came up with for the "new edition" of our family festival:

First, its established name would remain, to avoid confusion and to build on its equity (it still had some), but we've decided to add the word "new" to state clearly that something different is at hand. Now it's:

THE NEW CAPITAL CITY FAMILY FESTIVAL

— INVITES YOU TO HAVE —

THE TIME OF YOUR LIFE!

TARGET SPONSORS: (names may be trademarks or registered)[4]

Minute Maid orange juice and
    Coca-Cola, its parent company

Pastime Industries (child crafts)

Airline whose advertising emphasis
    is being on time

Minuteman Press (franchise)

Day & Night Air Conditioning

Seiko or Timex

Day Plastics (novelties)

Day International (art supplies)

Day Food Company (pizzas)

Time Sport USA

Time Warner Entertainment

Timeout (apparel)

ENTERTAINMENT: (either form our own, change existing names or bring in new)

Examples: Country group might be named or renamed BIG TIME COUNTRY, rock group named with some "in" time-related phrasing popular that year; parade of strolling entertainers for children, THE TIME-PASSERS; nostalgia group, MOMENTS FROM YESTERDAY, etc.

DECORATIONS

Beds of perennials (four o'clocks) in the shape of clock faces (really telling time?) and hour glasses; friendly clock faces (festival logo for that year) on all graphics; calendar pages for printed programs and stationery; huge count-down-to-Day-One calendar on site or at busy downtown location; etc. Have T- (for Time)-Shirts printed with the clock face, twelve "times" from which to choose, then announce the "Hour Winner" on each hour, a different time chosen throughout the day; those wearing t-shirts with the announced hour win small prizes and become eligible for a big drawing.

AREA AND ELEMENT NAMING

Main Stage: PRIME TIME-STAGE

Stage Two: BIG TIME STAGE

Stage Three: COUNTRY *HEAR* AND NOW STAGE

Entrance Path: THE WALK-IN TIME

Pedestrian Paths: TICK-TOCK CLOCK BLOCK (leads to the JUST A LITTLE TIME kids area); FUNTIME WALK; NEW CENTURY STREET; *WATCH* YOUR STEP LANE (Okay, lighten up)

Food Area: CENTURY 21 FEAST

Trash Receptacles: WASTE OF TIME (now stay with me)

Sports/Games Area: PLAY-TIME

Merchandise Area: JUST BUYING TIME

Shuttle Service: TIME AND AGAIN trips

Portable Restroom Area: TIME OUT-HOUSES

Had enough? Get the idea?

As you begin to respond to the RFP you've chosen, remember this approach. It'll make your project design lots more fun and much more appealing to those for whom you're designing it.

To really impress me (remember, I've issued your RFP) you might fully develop two or three themes for consideration. Always, when you give more in response than the RFP requested, you're bound to make a better impression and to improve your chances of being chosen over any competitors who stay strictly within the given RFP boundaries.

THE CASE OF THE OLD-SHOE HANG-AROUNDS

"Okay," you say, "you've made this big issue out of event cosmetics. You say events have to look good to be good. Then how do you account for some events that are uglier than homemade sin and still pack 'em in year after year?"

Note, if you will, that virtually all of those surviving bashed and battered relics are really quite old. They don't only *look* old, they *are* old. Furthermore, those ancients are almost always ones that have returned to the same site year after year for decades, with very little change in content or format. Best examples: county and state fairs, events featuring livestock in some way, vehicle races (usually drag), and demolition derbies.

Through the aging process, these old timers have invoked the "forced tradition" privilege, which now means *keep your hands off and your changes to yourself.* I had the temerity—the gall!—to suggest a few years ago that a popular state fair ("It's the ugliest thing I've every seen.") be leveled and a beautiful, well-planned version with imaginative architecture and an efficient crowd-flow pattern be built in its place.

I nearly had to enter the witness protection program.

These old-timers have earned their right to exist, through support by such fierce, almost maniacal, bands of followers that there's no way to get to them to bring about any "improvements."

Don't let these oldies-goodies sway you from your looking-good goal, however. Their longevity is the reason for their survival; it's not an excuse for "Nouveau Ugly."

AND FINALLY . . .

Clothes may or may not make the person, but proper "clothing"— its overall pleasant presence—goes a long way to making an event *really special*. And if atmosphere is thirty percent of fine dining (the other two-thirds being quality of food and the at-table company), then it's at least that percentage in its contributions to better happenings. Regardless of its size, your event should be special, or you shouldn't be having it. You can help make it so with the right outward appearance.

Always remember: in special events, presentation may not be everything, *but it's sure plenty big!*

Notes

[1]This chapter is an expansion of the "Poor Physical Condition" section, Chapter Four, *SE:IO*.

[2]For more on sponsorship, see Chapters 7-10, *SE:IO*.

[3]Sonotube® is a registered trademark of Sonoco, Inc. For dealer information, call 1-800-532-8248.

[4]An excellent source for potential sponsor names, products and addresses is the two-volume publication, *Companies and Their Brands*, A Gale Trade Names Directory, 835 Penobscot Building, Detroit, MI 48226-4094. This source is usually available in larger libraries. Also, see *SE:IO* for additional sponsor sources and information on sponsorships.

Chapter Four

PUMPING UP
MARKETING MUSCLES[1]

Dictionary definition: MARKETING—the act of buying or selling in a market.

Well . . . yes. But this is more what we should keep in mind in the event context, since we'll be giving *good* marketing a great deal of attention:

(GOOD) MAR•KET•ING, (MÄR´KI TING) *n.*—Pro-active programs—such as advertising, publicity, product packaging, promotions, sponsorship, sales, bannering, speeches, Internet and faxes – all or some of which work together to generate interest and a desire to take some pre-designated action by a specified group of people.

In short, TELL 'EM AND SELL 'EM. Shorter still, Tell/Sell.

Obviously, marketing an event, regardless of its size, is a big essential. If that's so, then why does the events industry suffer such widespread atrophy of its marketing muscles?

There are three primary causes:

1. POOR RECOGNITION OF MARKETING IMPORTANCE

Events are products. And just like toothpaste, vacuum cleaners and new cars, *they have to be marketed.* People cannot or will not buy into them unless they know about them and are convinced to attend or participate in them.

Too few eventers recognize or give proper weight to marketing. Evidence of this fact is the too-frequent practice of rewarding Mrs. Nicelady or Mr. Hardworker with the title of "PR Chairholder," "Publicity Director" or "Media Coordinator" as reward for contributions in time and effort (and maybe money) to the event.

"After all, they *do* deserve some recognition, like a title with a job that's not too demanding."

> **There is no event job more demanding, more important,**
>
> **than that of selling the event!**

Frequently, the closest Nicelady and Hardworker have come to media releases, promotional concepts or advertising campaigns is the mention of such in their company staff meetings. They often don't have any idea even where to start. Or, especially, how to finish the job.

2. "MARKETING" IS A BLURRED WORD

Surprising numbers of people aren't even sure what "marketing" *really* means. Obviously, event managers can't get it done unless they know what "that committee" is supposed to do. Even if marketing or any of its components are not your shtick, as a current or potential member of the special events community, you should have more than a cursory understanding of its workings and importance, sooner or later.

As a volunteer you'll have at least *some* dealings with those in your marketing arm. (If you don't, something's wrong.) Should you be a paid manager or an executive volunteer, you will likely have considerable interaction with marketing. (If you don't, something's *really* wrong!)

You can better perform your input as a "feeder" in the marketing effort if you have a working comprehension of what marketing does, and why. Hopefully, by the end of this chapter, you will have a clearer idea of what marketing is and how to make it work for an event.

3. MARKETING IS GIVEN A TOO-LOW PRIORITY

Largely due to Causes 1 & 2 above, too few bucks are budgeted for marketing. So many other things always seem to come first. This practice also reflects a peculiar, fairly common, difficult-to-justify, practice of many companies: When those firms get into financial trouble, they usually down-size the sales force and marketing department first. Explain that.

And now, one-by-one, I'll try to apply each marketing discipline to events, hoping to help both you and/ or your marketing squad function with high effectiveness.

JUST WHAT IS PUBLICITY?[2]

> **Obtaining time or space, *FREE OF CHARGE*, usually in news media, for the purpose of bringing a person, organization, event, thing, philosophy, image, cause, or other matter to the attention of the general public or segment thereof. Effective publicity has a specified, predetermined goal to direct its strategy. Most often, publicity appears *within the* editorial format *of both print and* broadcast media.**

In nearly every case, publicity can see itself clearly as the most effective event marketing tool. It should, it has three "I's":

1.   It's **INEXPENSIVE**. You don't have to buy space or time to spread your message.

2.   It's **IMPACTFUL**. By the nature of its editorial context, publicity tends to have *credibility* with readers, listeners or viewers—often more so than advertising. Its editorial format can frequently lend the valuable quasi-endorsement of an ostensibly impartial third-party, i.e., the newspaper, television channel or radio station, which by the very act of carrying the message, buttresses its importance and pertinence.

3.   It's **IMPRESSIVE**. A stack of print, video and audio clips, none of which were time-purchased, can do a cracker-jack job of helping sell sponsorships, attract quality volunteers and negotiate some event-favorable contracts, especially with publicity-sensitive talent.

GETTING MEDIA COVERAGE

Life as an event publicist is very often a no-pain, no-gain exercise. Getting publicity is one of the toughest jobs in the events (or any other) industry. Media types are always aware that "flacks" are trying to finagle material into editorial formats as a means of engendering credibility and bypassing advertising costs. That fact, coupled with the astonishing competition for editorial space and time, means lots of hard work if a publicist is to be successful.

Those media people will also tell you that there's always a place for *good* (let me repeat, *good)* material. Fine, you say, but what is *good* material?

If you were to ask that question of fifty newspaper, television and radio representatives, you would likely get about forty-five different answers; it might actually be fifty out of fifty. Here's what you could be told:

SOME WILL TELL YOU TO:	OTHERS WILL TELL YOU TO:
call them first, then send your story	send in your story, never mind calling
come in to discuss material	don't come in, just send it
mail it, don't fax or e-mail it	fax it or e-mail it, don't mail it
use fax only	use e-mail only
ad nauseam	and *ad* some more *nauseam*

So what do you do? Well, you try to hit a medium. (I would have said *happy* medium, but many aren't all that happy.) Here are my suggestions for trying to please as many news people as possible.

WORKING REGULARLY WITH *SAME* CONTACTS

In most instances, as an event publicist, you will work very frequently with the same local media contacts with some regularity. It is to your advantage to get to know them well and to follow their wishes, which, by the way, have been known to change often, quickly and/or drastically. Versatility is right up there with creativity, planning, and writing abilities among the required assets of a publicist.

Regarding contacts, I have a dogmatic belief that their value to publicists is too often highly overrated. True, they can be useful. For one thing, you have easier access to them if they know who you are and, especially, if they appreciate the quality of your work. Maybe it's happened, but I have never personally known a media staffer who used publicity hand-outs only because he/she simply knew the publicist. Familiarity does not necessarily breed big-time coverage.

If your material is only of borderline quality (shame!), you *might* get pick-up because the media recipient knows and likes you. (Bet: it'll be heavily rewritten or prepared from scratch after questions, interviews and research.) But don't count on that good luck. Make your handouts of use-calibre quality. Always.

Some remarkable coverage I've seen over the years has been through media people the publicist did not know and who did not know the publicist. Such results came about because of the quality of material, its freshness, credible ideas and eye-comforting presentation format, coupled with good writing and careful timing.

You do not need to whine-wine-or-dine media folks every week to develop a relationship that will get your stuff used. Media people are incredibly busy every minute. Rarely do they have time just to sit around and make small talk over a couple of drafts. Always meet them on a business basis; if a social opportunity arises, it'll make itself known and you should take advantage of it.

HELP THEM DO THEIR JOBS

Absolutely the best way to curry media favor and, therefore, to build your good-contact base is *by always giving them high-grade, ready-to-use material.* These busy people learn quickly to love those who do as much of their work for them as possible.

Here are some hints I have found useful in several decades of work with media:

— **Spend your time wisely**. Learn quickly who the truly worthwhile names and positions are. If you know you should work with the entertainment editor, general-topic columnist, sports staff, feature writer, etc., concentrate on preparing material to their specifications.

— **Ask for an initial meeting**, seeking to find out *exactly* what each one wants, when they want it and how they want it prepared and delivered.

— When you have *good* reason to do so (deadlines are near and there's no time to wait for your material to get through the fax stax, or your contacts have asked you to come by), **take your material to them for an in-person review,** to determine what elucidation they may need.

— In most media centers today security is so tight that **you'll almost certainly need an appointment,** otherwise you'll probably just have to leave it at the front desk or with a security officer.

· If personal visits won't work, **fax or drop off the material anyway**. But be sure to allow plenty of time for it to find its way to the designated recipient, which can take several hours.

· **Let's consider faxing**. Some of my colleagues have declared that faxing is not acceptable to most media people. Not true. I media-fax upwards of forty or fifty documents to different media monthly and have done so for years. Not more than half-a-dozen times have I had recipients call me down for doing so or ask me to refrain. Maybe it's because I limit my output to appropriate subjects succinctly written on as few pages as possible, which I'll discuss further below. Every one of the many successes I've had the last five or six years in turning out media or getting coverage has resulted from faxed information.

· That brings up another important subject: **phone answering machines and services.** (For more on this important matter, see No. 9 in Chapter 7 below.) Obviously, today's miraculous technology is for the most part very beneficial. But sometimes it works against you as a publicist. Phone-answering systems are a boon in some cases, not-so-boon in others, such as when you're trying to reach media contacts. Only very, very rarely will your call be answered by the person you're calling and just as rarely will your call be returned, unless you've left a compact power message of a potency equal to "Houston, we have a problem." These systems, as never before, enable media reps to monitor their calls, so be sure you have something really important to put across and are truly adept at doing so in a few really fast seconds, or you're in trouble. Keep your messages very brief and packed with powerful, directly relevant words. And get ready to fax or drop off your information; that is almost always the response (if you get one) when you do make the connection.

WORKING REGULARLY WITH *DISTANT* CONTACTS

If you do your job well, you will constantly be looking for new paths to jog in your publicity fitness program. You will want to prepare and send specialized material to "new" media not in your immediate neighborhood, to support new sponsorship sales programs, swell tourism dollars and increase attendance, as well as to attract new talent and perhaps expand enrollment participation in competitions.

When you are working with new media contacts, your strategy must be basically different from that crafted for regular local contacts. Here are some suggestions:

— In preparing material, remember that those in this media category may know little or nothing about your event, its location and city, offerings, admission costs, parking facilities, special out-of-town guest services, etc. Make your material more detailed than its hometown versions.

— You might refer to the venue as "the sports center" for local consumption because nearly everyone knows it by that designation but put yourself In recipients' circumstances and frames of reference in another market; you know nothing but you need to know just about everything. For those distant media, then, you must refer to that sports facility by its official, phone-book-listed name, also giving its address, phone/fax numbers and clear directions to it.

— Ask yourself this mega-important question and answer it in media material formats:

> # What does our event have to offer that is powerful enough
>
> # to be of sufficient interest to people several miles distant,
>
> # things big enough to make them leave their homes
>
> # and drive, ride or fly to our happening?

If you come up with a zero answer, you might bring up this matter at the next event planning session, suggesting that ideas be explored for expansion of interest beyond your city boundaries. But if you have nothing to offer non-locals, don't waste your time or money with out-of-market media attempts.

— Too often you may not be able to establish direct contact or ongoing working relationships with distant media. Therefore, if your material has to be of touchdown quality with locals, it has to go the extra point for the outsiders.

WORKING WITH LOCAL *AND* DISTANT MEDIA

— *Please don't fax* your black-and-white glossies or color negatives. They just don't fax too well. (Oh, yes, some do try it!) *Drop off, messenger* or *mail* all artwork in clearly marked DO NOT BEND OR FOLD packs.

— About artwork—photos, drawings, maps, illustrations, etc. Unless yours is a large, big-budgeted happening, it's likely you'll have to depend on the generosity of professional photographers and artists, ideally serving in a sponsor capacity. Otherwise, you'll probably have to rely on well-meaning amateurs, but try to avoid doing so. All too rarely is such material of pride quality. If you have something really worthwhile for camera reporting, attempt to lure the local videographer and newspaper photogs to do it. If you need artwork, approach instructors at high schools, colleges or art studios, asking if, under their close supervision, students might fulfill your need. Their photo/video departments might also help.

— More about artwork. Please don't fold or staple it—ever! Amazingly, editors do from time to time receive eight-by-ten-inch photos neatly folded to fit snugly in number ten business-type envelopes. And the caption is stapled inside photo margins. Those who do these things are immediately labeled "A" for Amateur . . . a put-down that is *very* difficult to erase.

— Still a little more about artwork. If you are going to provide it, especially photos, you must know the format each primary news-user requires. Some will take, some won't take: Poloroids®, black-and-whites, color slides and transparencies, negatives and videos.

— Finally, about artwork. Don't try to crop your art with scissors or the tear-with-a-ruler technique. This is not good. Send quality photos and your media experts will know how to make them fit. Or they'll come out and shoot their own.

EFFORT . . . AS IN HARD WORK

Never has an event pleased all its people all the time. And no event publicist has ever pleased all his/her media people all the time, either. It can be done on a probability basis of about once every other century. So don't get discouraged if you or your marketing committee don't score with every try—or even most them. In publicity, "some of the time" can be considered quite successful. Occasionally, even "once" can be an earned source of pride.

There are many factors governing the acceptance of publicity material, along with its quality. For one there is just so much time and space available for news in every medium every day. Coverage chances shrivel for the lighter and happier material on an event when there is a big-time sports annual or quadrennial spectacle, a particularly mind-staggering terrorist bombing or a major celebrity murder trial. (A mid-90s court hearing—a monstrous media time and space eater—was called "the trial of the century." That's because it seemed like it took a century to get through it.)

Timing and non-specific, often inaccurate addressing on the part of the publicity operation are often big problems. You can have the best material ever produced, but if it gets there too early or too late, goes to the wrong people or "desk" (sports desk, features desk, etc.), or thanks to out-of-date software, is addressed to a long-dead media recipient, it's just so many useless images on paper.

But one of the most pervasive problems is *the lack of something really news- or feature-worthy to cover*. This is one of the most frequent complaints I hear from media reps vis-à-vis special event coverage. Doing the same thing year after year, never bringing in something new that's substantial enough in its inherent quality to interest media—this is the core of the problem.

Another aspect, however, is that event publicists often don't use their creative imaginations to develop heretofore untouched feature subjects or bring new life to topics not covered in several years. Events are people, and people make news and features. It's just a matter of finding a hook to snag media coverage.

POINTS ON PUBLICIZING YOUR EVENT

Based on many years of enjoying dual careers, one in special events, the other in general and event marketing with an emphasis on publicity, I will offer the following observations for those who want to magnetize event media coverage. You will find a goodly number of my colleagues differing with me on some of these suggestions, but I stand by my words.

I'll delve into writing content later in this chapter, when we look at making media visits to your event effective and productive. But I'm going to start with the cosmetics of your material. After all, before a word is read, the way your writings look have created an impression. To make it a good one, try these recommendations:

— **Your material must please the eye *at very first glance*.** When media people pick up your document, even before they read it, a flick of an opinion has formed. And it's the start of a decision that might consign your material to the "To Be Used" basket or to the round-file. If your media kit weighs about the same as a healthy newborn hippo, you've got a weighty problem. If it is a sheath of wall-to-wall, single-spaced copy with less than .0000000023% white space, your problem just doubled. And if you've saved paper by printing front and back, your chiefs should put you in a job where you'll do less damage to your event.

— Now, here's where I'm going to generate more heat from some of my colleagues: **I believe the media release, per se, will be a 20ᵗʰ Century has-been** as we move farther into the Years 2000. Many *event* publicists won't admit it, but it's generally a long time between verbatim pick-ups of event media releases, except in the cases of small-staffed publications (usually weeklies). In recent years, I have used the media release frequently as a sales tool for sponsorships more than for its more conventional purpose. Well written releases (see samples at the end of this chapter) are dramatic supports that can have effective impact on potential sponsors.

— If not releases, then what? ***Fact sheets, that's what!*** Effective publicists, especially those in the events industry, are often having far better success with fact sheets than with media releases. (On occasion, the two work well together, especially when dealing with a mix of metros, trade and weeklies having limited-size staffs). And fact sheets are just as workable, perhaps more so, with the electronic media folks, who often seem to prefer them to publicist-prepared scripts. Here are pointers on fact sheet construction (see sample at the end of this chapter):

√ *Limit them to two pages.* "What! I can't get everything about my festival on two sheets," you sob. In most cases you can, if you discipline yourself to putting down only the most power-packed words to create only the most meaningful messages. In fact sheets – in nearly all media documents – the big failing of many publicists are their attempts to get too much in them. Don't.

√ *Make it a **fact** sheet.* Leave out the kindest, truest, greatest, most dazzling, absolutely the finest, the first time in recorded history, the biggest of its type, most wonderful and unbelievable, fascinating and magnificent event in the cosmos. In the first place, it probably isn't true; in the second, even if it were, editors have been largely so desensitized to those words, they simply don't believe them and can get very irritated by being force-fed them. If things are truly great, let the *facts* prove it. Follow this advice and you will also significantly reduce your wordage and fact-sheet length at the same time.

√ If, after really trying, you become convinced that you cannot produce a two sheeter, *think about dividing your huge, gray-page opus into two or three individual-subject, more reader-friendly fact sheets.* Most often media people are interested in tightly-specific subjects. Put one or two together that deal *only* with event "sub-topics," such as food, entertainment, guest accommodations, activity schedules, special ceremonies, VIP's and celebrities, etc. If they need more than one fact sheet, that need will become instantly obvious. Make a good impression by just happening to have others within arm's reach.

√ *Really well-prepared, eye-friendly, truly creative fact sheets* are often more likely to seize attention than many other types of documents. In this age of incomprehensible levels of competition for every inch of paper and each broadcast second, *you had better be creative* or you'll run right off the Information Highway into the Information Junk Yard quicker than you can double-click your mouse. Remember, you have, at best, *two seconds* to outdo your competition for an editor's attention when he/she takes your material from an in-box stack not affectionately known as "The Leaning Tower." If your material looks blah, it stands big chances of going into the blah wastebasket, along with all other blah, blah-plus, maxi blah and ultra-blah items. Maybe even before it has been fully read.

√ *How do you format a survivor-class fact sheet?* Start with a smack-'em-over-the-head heading that would make *anyone* want to know more so that your recipients are forced to read on by the sheer power of ravenous curiosity. Have an out-of-body experience; step "outside" and ask yourself what message about your subject would so tantalize you that you absolutely could not resist reading on to find out what your fact sheet is all about. Now, condense your thought to about fifteen forceful words—and voilá! You have your mighty heading. Just one more thing: put it in large enough letters that it can be read from about five feet away. In the event that it's posted on an assignment board, it will attract plenty of attention.

√ *Be sure your fact sheet appeals to the eye*, is succinctly written and well organized—*with creative subheadings* (do not use the entirely unimaginative yawn-makers "who," "what," "when," "where," and "how"). If lots of white space further encourages reading, it's very likely to get at least a once-over . . . maybe even a twice-over . . . *maybe even used!*

ADVICE ON ADVISORIES

— **Media advisories** (some prefer "alerts"), issued to entice media to cover some activity firsthand, are one of the most abused exercises in the event publicist's workout routine. If a Chairholder is expected to bang his or her gavel three times instead of two, bam! Out with an advisory, promising a history-making photo op! But creatively structured and properly used—*and dealing with a subject that truly has media appeal* —the advisory can be an awe-inspiring marketing muscle-builder. I should emphasize that advisories are just as subject to competition for initial attention as are fact sheets and media releases. Here are some suggestions that may help you produce workable advisories:

√ *Keep these to one page only.* (Yes, you can, too, get all your information on a single sheet!) And pick up your "look" from your fact sheet—very arresting heading, well fashioned format, *concise* facts, and knock-out, can't-miss-it-size vital information—what, where, exactly when, why (if necessary)—and *plenty of white space!* (How many times do I have to repeat that?) Most of my successes have resulted from what I call "the flier format," which I developed several years ago (see sample at the end of this chapter).

√ *Timing advisories is crucial.* Knowing that I rarely have a subject that can compete effectively with the latest congressional misdeed, serial crime celebrity or contradictory medical finding, I don't go out with it well ahead of the happening. It invariably gets lost or "was never received."

My first advisory (maximum: two per subject) is faxed three to five days ahead, with a reminder version being faxed the day before *or even early the morning of,* if it takes place late morning or afterwards. On the very infrequent occasions I have an opportunity that really is a biggie, I notify recipients by their voice mail eight to ten days ahead, going out immediately with a faxed fact sheet and one initial advisory, followed by a last-minute reminder version of that advisory.

WE HAVE TO START MEETING LIKE THIS

Media Conferences. Ah, yes, *media conferences!*

√ If, in the subject at hand, you can come pretty close to offering an equivalent to the Second Coming, *call a media conference.* An announcement of the use of a roll of Duct® tape does not qualify —unless it is the fifty-millionth roll to be used by your event and you have created a media/crowd spectacular to commemorate the occasion.

√ To determine whether something is worth a media conference, if the answer to most or all the following questions is "yes," you can *think* about calling one:

- Is it *really* important, something of truly major significance?

- Is the subject too detailed or otherwise not suited to stand alone as a subject in a release, fact sheet or one-on-one interview?

- Does it require the credibility of on-site quotes from a spokesperson?

- Does it need to be demonstrated, explained by an expert, unveiled, assembled or otherwise "handled" to be well understood by media?

- Must there be an opportunity for a face-to-face question/answer exchange between media and source, to clarify points or avoid misunderstandings?

- Is the nature of photo/video potentials such that media should cover firsthand with their own cameras?

ANATOMY OF A MEDIA CONFERENCE

Below are what I've found to be fourteen sure-fire guides to help carry off a successful gathering of invited media. Fortunately, most often the conference you will call will be on a positive subject; however, you may have to assemble one to deal with a negative, regrettable subject. In either case, these guidelines apply.

1. Check with a good media contact to determine whether your preferred timing will bump up against a biggie news-break. Another suggestion is to contact your local Associated Press office to see what you'd be up against in their daybook schedule. Then, of course, set your timing accordingly.

2. My personal preference, all other things being equal, is to set *all* media events, including conferences, on a Tuesday, Wednesday or Thursday. Ideal time is usually between 9:30 and 11:30 a.m. This lets television crews get back to their stations in time for segments to be edited for late afternoon and early evening newscasts.

3. The perfect location for that conference:

— is as near as possible to media centers. However, if there is a widely spread pattern of those locations, then hold it as close as you can to a convergence of major thoroughfares or expressways. Just be sure you choose a location probably familiar to media or which is very easily located on a municipal map. If necessary, include a well-drawn map or clearly described directions with your announcement material.

— has sufficient *reserved* parking for all media and participants reasonably close to the conference room proper. When necessary, media aides to greet arrivals and conduct them to the conference site.

— provides directional signs, also welcome by arriving media.

— is quiet, all unrelated sound being shut out—no telephones to warble, PA announcements, office machine and personnel noises, street racket, etc.

— has a media-directed background to the "staging area" that is attractive and photogenic; sometimes a company banner is used to promote identity and facilitate image in photos and videos. You have been *very* careful not to clutter the backdrop, which will detract from the presider. That means you've avoided multi-color plaids behind Mafia funeral-calibre banks of flowers, the flags of all nations recognized by the U.S., and poster-size framed photos of your entire executive staff.

— offers comfortable chairs at tables, thus facilitating writing and recording machines. Theatre-style seating is acceptable.

— allows *plenty* of space surrounding the presider(s) and the room periphery to facilitate quick and easy movements of still photographers and videographers.

4. Select the best person to be the pivotal informant. He/she should be the most knowledgeable on the subject, whether that person is top banana or one of the bunch. Too often, when the presider is chosen by uppity title rather than upper competency, the primary conference product is tongue-tumbled embarrassment. It's the same pain suffered when barely lucid auto dealers insist on being stars in their own television commercials, just because they're paying the bills.

> A personal belief/professional comment: I have always felt that PR people or publicists should generally *not* be conference spokespersons. By the very nature of their professions—paid public advocates of those they represent—their comments are at least somewhat suspect, their credibility most likely a bit sagging. Only exception: those very rare instances when conferences deal with the subject of public or media relations.

5. You may need more than one source at a media conference. Your subject matter may be so broad ranging that it requires input from several specialists. This can make the conference especially interesting and successful. However, be sure to tap *one* person to be primary presider, to avoid confusion. That person should be in charge throughout the conference, calling on specialists to respond to appropriate questions.

6. Help all source providers thoroughly prepare themselves, especially for the Q&A segment. Practice with probable media questions and assist them in reducing responses to as few meaningful words as possible. Potent brevity is the stuff of sound bites, those few seconds of weighty quotes adored by TV, radio and print news editors, which means those words have a good chance of being aired or printed.

7. Prepare all hand-outs along the lines suggested earlier in this chapter. Include thumbnail biogs on all presiders—professional backgrounds, position with the organization and subject on which that person is most knowledgeable vis-à-vis the media conference.

8. Have photos available of persons conducting the conference. Ideally, there should be available one action shot and one head-and-shoulders print of each participant.

9. If appropriate, you might install the "Information Buffet" (See p. 61f) at the media conference.

10. Start the conference on time, unless you have good reason to believe important reps will be a few minutes late; a ten-minute-late start is barely tolerable for punctual media, but wait absolutely no longer for their tardy colleagues, who can get after-conference shots and statements on their own.

11. Unless there are really extraordinary circumstances, a media conference, including statement and Q&A, should run absolutely no longer than twenty to thirty minutes.

12. Publicist should take a pre-determined signal from the presider, denoting termination of Q&A, or the publicist, noting that media questions are beginning to get "reachy" or "thin," should end the session.

13. Arrange for presider(s) to remain afterwards for a few minutes, to allow for individual questions some media don't want to share with their competitors.

14. You and all source participants should stay close to telephones the remainder of the day, being prepared to handle clarification calls from media.

What should you do when that publicist's nightmare—the no-show media conference—happens? Swallow hard, get rid of the red in your face, and move on. There is life after a media conference attended only by absentees; I know . . . been there, done that. You might get in your car or call a messenger and get the conference material to most appropriate media, but don't count on volumes of usage. It just almost never happens.

AVOID TUBE-APHOBIA

Perhaps because of its enormous visual impact and exceptional popularity, television seems to scare the dickens out of many publicists. That's foolish. Even more than other media, TV is a ravenous consumer of information, especially since so many stations carry many hours of news and features daily. TV people will tell you that they can use as much (here's that word again!) *good* material as you can provide them. And preparing TV material and activity isn't all that difficult.

To start with, look for opportunities with movement and color. Talking heads in white shirts and black coats aren't too visually appealing on the tube. In most events, finding some animated opportunities shouldn't be too difficult. If you have trouble finding them, you may need to exercise more creativity or your event's buried 'way too deep in the boring bin. In either case, work needs to be done.

You'll generally be better off convincing television of something valuable enough to cover and having their cameras do the filming with staff audio, rather than trying to produce air-quality segments with camcorders in less than talented hands. Your well-crafted advisories and fact sheets should do the trick.

MEDIA AT YOUR EVENT

Successful work with media on site starts with doing everything possible to make their jobs as easy and quick as possible. Here are several suggestions that nearly always work:

— Have *very knowledgeable* people on hand to serve as media hosts or assistants. If your event isn't large enough to justify a corps of media aides, that being their only assignments, then have other, fully-prepared people who can break away from primary responsibilities standing at-ready when media do show.

— Take media to the best sources for information, to those who really know the area-of-topic. Skip Pat Pessimist, however, who never says a good word about anything, even though he/she may be quite knowledgeable about certain areas or subjects.

— Have good, *fresh* material on hand—and let the media select their own. Don't hand them handfuls of documents they already have or those they can't use; put out new stuff, even if it's a deftly spruced-up rewrite.

— If you have a real out-of-the-ordinary request for which you are simply unprepared, again use those magic words, "I don't know, but I'll look into it." Then do so. Right then and there, get an answer—if there is one. If there is no satisfactory response at hand, own up to it and say you'll continue to look into it.

"INFORMATION BUFFET" AT MEDIA HEADQUARTERS

My favorite way to "serve" media material is with an "Information Buffet." In a media-friendly location, I place as many skirted tables as needed, putting on them separated stacks of releases, fact sheets, photos, schedules, advisories, biographies, maps and schematics, etc. (Sponsor material may also be included.)

At the "starting point" of the table, I place the "plates," which are media kit folders or envelopes. Reps then visit tables as often as they like, picking up only what is of specific interest to them and stuffing their own kits. Tables should be checked frequently to be sure that there is a plentiful supply of all items.

Events make lots of media friends with well-operated media headquarters. If your event is of a size or appeal to draw regularly eight or ten or more media reps, try the following guidelines for your media headquarters. For fewer reps, be sure you give them lots of personal attention, even if you cannot justify a fully operational media center (Cro-Magnons still call them press rooms), which should offer the following attributes:

— **Locate and staff it so that *media only* use it**. Do not mix any other group with media. Ever.

— **Position the Information Buffet** or document tables where especially easy access is assured and so that media will clearly understand what's available and how to use the buffet.

— **Keep the Buffet tables well stocked** with up-to-date material, high-quality still color and black-and-white photos, etc. If you're really big—and rich—include video clips.

— In a corner, **create a lounge,** with comfortable borrowed or rented chairs or couches and a table with coffee, tea, fruit and soft drinks, pastries, paper plates and cups. Again, if you're really big and wealthy, provide a breakfast, lunch and dinner food buffet as well.

— **Arrange for *fully secure* storage facilities** to accommodate cameras and other costly paraphernalia media folks might like to leave safely behind as they scout your event for stories . . . or simply go out to enjoy it.

— For larger media headquarters, **have two or three very well-trained media aides on hand** during operating hours. Should you be blessed by major network camera crews, reporter-photog teams from national newspapers or perhaps some syndicated columnists, put your best media aides with each. Most media crews prefer to work with one aide only during their visits, providing he/she is of top quality.

— **Easily available telephones, fax machines, word-processor computers, electric typewriters and photocopiers are essential** in a well-planned media center. If your budget is tight, look into borrowing or renting this equipment, or get it through suppliers free under a sponsorship arrangement.

— Truly large, high-appeal **events should have interview alcoves** adjacent to the main media center, with attractive backdrops that include the event name in camera-angled position. (See Anatomy of a Media Conference above for guidelines in setting up workable interview areas p.58ff.)

— Within reason, **families and friends of working media should be accommodated** as if they were media themselves. If the foremost anchor person from a nightly national network newscast should show up with twenty or more friends and relatives, if you have more nerve than room in the center, ask half or all of them to leave. And then immediately resign your publicity post, change your name, put on a disguise and leave the country with no plans to return.

Am I saying media are and must be pampered? You got it!

CRISIS PUBLICITY

It's like having a serial-killer relative; you don't want to think about it, much less admit it or talk about it. But the situation *has* to be handled. Even the most nearly perfectly planned events can and often will suffer crises—dangerous weather, injurious or fatal accident, fire, heart attack . . . even murder, or God forbid, a terrorist attack (see p.94f).

You the publicist are responsible for that part of the overall crisis plan (*and every event MUST have one— a WRITTEN one*) that deals with media involvement in crises. Here are some guidelines to help publicity units formulate such a plan:

—Take the offensive when a serious matter occurs.

Admittedly there can be an acre or two of gray area between "non-serious" and "serious." Only you and event officials can decide on this question at the time of occurrence. This decision must often be made in a matter of a very few minutes. By passive reaction, it could appear as if the event may have something to hide or is afraid for some other mysterious reason to face questioning. Pro-action can also make media friendships that last well beyond the emergency. Pick up the phone and notify all media at the outset of the crisis in as rapid succession as possible. And throughout the duration of the episode, when you are given new information *and the authorization to release it* (see below), again take the initiative and provide that information to all media.

—Tell only the truth about what you *know* to be fact.

Never, under even the most pressing circumstances, offer an opinion, possibility, probability, or a hearsay tidbit. Tell media only what you *know* to be absolute fact. Never should you, as a publicist, fear to *proudly* use this response—

I DON'T KNOW.

You'll be amazed at how that will enhance your credibility. It may not initially please media, but so be it. Frowns are better at the moment than tears later in a courtroom. Try to follow "I don't know" with "but I'll try to find out," *if* you feel that a response is possible, appropriate and safe. Always carry through with that promise, getting back to the requester as soon as you possibly can, regardless of your response.

—Follow every order, direction or suggestion from emergency officials.

At the first opportunity, identify yourself to emergency officials – police, sheriffs, medical personnel, firefighters, etc. Tell them you need to know *exactly* what you may tell media, and indicate you'll be happy to work on their behalf with news people and will always check information or requests with authorized sources. But remember, their first duty is the safety of any people and property involved. Often they may not have time to respond to your needs, so stay out of their way until a clear moment clearly occurs.

If severe injury or death has occurred, refer all media inquiries to the emergency team or its spokesperson for details. You may release victim information *only after you have been fully authorized to do so by the designated authority.* In virtually every case however, that kind of information should and will come first and perhaps only from law enforcement sources. It could be several days (and, therefore, probably news valueless) before you can disseminate such information. Tough.

—Ideally, there should always be one spokesperson on behalf of an event.

Confusion or worse is almost always the result when more than one voice speaks publicly during a volatile or sensitive circumstance. Determine in your long-range crisis planning, which should include your legal consultant and representatives of local emergency services, who that one spokesperson will be, whether it's you, the event Chairholder, executive director, board chair—whomever. Be sure to name a responsible person you *know* will always be on site or entirely accessible at all hours. Then let the entire organization know in meetings and/or by written word who that person is (along with his/her phone numbers) and the requirement that the named person *only* will serve as crisis spokesperson.

—Write it down.

Put your information on paper as quickly as possible after a serious happening—and, at every opportunity, issue printed statements instead of or immediately after verbal disclosures. This advice covers the post-crisis well-it's-all-over announcement.

> ## DON'T PANIC!
> Hysteria is more contagious than a cold at preschool. Keep your cool.

POWER WRITING

We've considered how to assist media in many situations, the way material should look and how to get it to the right recipients in a planned, effective manner. Let's now consider the *contents* of your media messages. And incidentally, just maybe, these approaches might help in other written communications as well.

As I mentioned in the preface, "Power Writing" is the term I apply to the concept that *placement* of words on a page and their *positioning* in phrases, sentences, paragraphs and larger partitions are as important as their literal and "emotional" definitions. (Literal: wrong—erroneous, incorrect, inaccurate, improper, etc.; Emotional: *WRONG!— You're an idiot, you stupid fool! You're totally out of it! You don't know what you're talking about!*)

Agreeable to English instructors is the fact that every hard-and-fast rule of effective formal writing must be entirely mastered before Power Writing can be attempted. You must know really well exactly what you're doing before you can stop doing it and start doing something else. Suggestion: therefore, if you're taking English courses, do not introduce Power Writing in your next essay or exam.

Vastly disagreeable to English instructors is the fact that Power Writing throws out *many* of those hard-and-fast formal rules—and doesn't bother replacing them with any *new* rules, hard and/or fast . . . or even soft and slow.

> **POWER WRITING is an acquired sense of documented communication that is effective, productive, super clear, reasonably brief, dramatic and eye-apealing.**

These qualities are objectives. As is true of any communication, including formal prose, Power Writing is never perfect. Nor does it suit every communications circumstance and need.

And it's not all that new . . .

— Everybody knows Suti and Hor, architects to Egyptian Pharoah Amenhotep III (1500-1400 B.C.), all but household names today, who stood the ancient world on end with their blazing sentence fragment, "Creator uncreated."

— Poets are also frequent practitioners. From Lord Byron, not better known as George Noel Gordon, who used not one but *two* consecutive sentence fragments (all right, exclamations) separated only by a tiny comma: "The isles of Greece, the isles of Greece!" Breathtaking. ("The isles of Greece – what?")

— Advertising copy producers are the foremost modern artisans of Power Writing, having very little space available to sell big-money cars, computers, video cameras and condos. Every word—and the spaces between them—must count.

This communications technique gratifies and complements our life and business styles on the threshold of the 21st Century. We are barraged by more messages in a given day than hit our parents in a month. Maybe two. And we have about a tenth the time to consider it, much less absorb and utilize it. If we want to make a marketing splash in this daily flood of words, we eventers had better do better than other word-makers.

AN ASIDE: I've noted that condensation is the very essence of Power Writing. At this moment, you're thinking, "If brevity is such a fundamental, why isn't this book briefer?" Believe it or not, it is. That is, it is considerably more condensed than it would have been had I chosen the formal or the more standard, instructive, how-to style. It would have had somewhat fewer pages, but the big difference would have been in the word count. I conservatively estimate that it has 20% to 30% fewer words than had I used more traditional writing styles. Be thankful.

MEDIA AND POWER WRITING

Why do I break into my how-to event narrative to provide a lesson in Power Writing? Because news media are the primary developers and users of this technique. It is necessitated out of the preciousness of air time and print space, in which news has to be provided in the fewest possible, most dynamic words.

In practicing Power Writing, consider these characteristics:

— **Sentence fragments are not only permissible**, they can be dynamic statements, far more potent than as sentence segments. But to make them more forceful, they should be used sparingly. By the way, periods are used to indicate the end of a sentence fragment. Sometimes.

— **Bullet points,** often really nothing more than long sentence fragments, are frequently much more forceful than the paragraphs or sentences they replace. I've often used bullet points in this book, denoted by numbering, use of "the dot" (•), em dashes (—) or other printer's "wingdings." Most are sentence fragments, but many are full sentences, when that seems called for.

— **Lots of white space**, created by avoiding lots of gray printing by using hanging indentions and segment separations, is a particularly important characteristic. It plays a big role in encouraging readership.

— In Power Writing, **paragraphs are not determined by subject matter,** nor do they usually have introductory sentences, exposition or development and closing summary sentences, as in formal writing. Rather, they are determined by length. Thick, "gray" paragraphs discourage the eye and often hinder reading. As a result, longer ones are very infrequently used in most modern channels of communications, especially newspapers and some magazines. Other excellent examples: printed or videotaped commercials, where only a few lines or seconds are available to get across a sell message.

— **Usually two or three simple sentences or one or two complex or compound sentences make up the typical Power Written paragraph.** (Sentence fragments, too, although for media, they usually take the form of bullet points.) This is because about four typewritten lines within margins equivalent to ten and seventy-five on a typewriter produce approximately one inch of standard newspaper column copy.

— In addition to assisting clarity, **punctuation in Power Writing enjoys the added property of imparting dramatic richness to writing.** Example: Ellipsis points (. . .) are not always used to indicate context omissions as in formal writing; instead, they sometimes introduce an expressive "eye-pause" to a phrase. Ditto for the dash, which is a "faster pause" than ellipsis points.

— As in good formal writing, **this contemporary style utilizes crisp, colorful verbs and solid adjectives** (no weak, tired exaggerations, superlatives or other tripe).

Further words about verbs: If you're not sure what "crisp, colorful" verbs are, you can get an idea just by paying attention to the next sports broadcast reporting baseball scores. You'll hear a bunch including: lost, won, beat, trounced, edged, clobbered, toppled, topped, squeezed, pounded, battered, bashed, walloped, mauled, bounced, creamed, spanked, smacked, cuffed, TKO'ed, pummeled, squeaked by, conquered, overwhelmed, shut out, sank, upset, dropped, whipped, etc. Just plain "won" or "lost" aren't colorful or crisp enough, especially when repeated many times during a newscast.

Or note the comma-less litany of your favorite aerobics instructor: "And stretch and pull and again and work and sweat now hurt and cry and again and groan now moan and reach just grind and push and . . ."

— Power writing is made even more powerful by use of this bit of information: **the *last* word or strongly connected group of words in a sentence or fragment and paragraph are the most impactful**; the *first* word or strongly-connected words are second in strength. Note:

> **Flab:** It was at 10 a.m. this morning that the River City Festival's ten-millionth guest was welcomed.

> **Muscle:** River City Festival today welcomed its ten-millionth guest.

> **Flab:** If the reader checks this book to see if I followed this suggestion in every case, he/she may find several exceptions here and there.

> **Muscle:** Reader, take a hike.

Try Power Writing in your media communications. You might like it. And so will "they."

HOW TO MEASURE PUBLICITY'S VALUE

Can't be done.

"You mean, after all that work you described above, we can't measure how effective publicity might be?"

Sorry, it's true. At least not on a workable, accurate, quantitative, meaningful basis.

I'm devoting space to this matter because you or your event publicity people almost surely will encounter requests—maybe demands—for publicity impact measurements, from sponsors or event directors. In the interest of satisfying a sponsor, you may *have* to participate in this stupidity. My hope is that this message (for many other believers in its futility) will get through to the right people to help stamp out this gross waste of time. And I certainly hope *you* won't ever impose this ridiculous practice on anyone—ever!

Every so often, I run across what is purported to be—*finally!*—THE be-all-and-end-all formula for accurately measuring the effectiveness of media coverage, formulas for giving it quantitative values. And every one of those methods so far has turned out to be convoluted, contrived, often humorous—and virtually entirely worthless . . . for the not-easily-duped.

It's shocking to see some of America's otherwise most forward-driven companies entering the 21st Century still trying to put an advertising value on publicity, a method that went out of style, for the most part, with disco. I thought *everyone* had finally admitted that trying to fix advertising-dollar figures to publicity space was a completely meaningless exercise. Here's why:

Suppose you buy a print ad or TV commercial time that says, "Our festival is the greatest, most stupendous, famous, glorious, grand, impressive, outstanding, remarkable and sublime special event in history." Those words appear in the ad format – an advertising-labeled rectangle in print, or the obvious commercial segment on TV or radio.

Now, suppose the *same meaning* (though likely not the same words) of that message turns up in the editorial columns (the "news" part) of print media or within the program or newscast framework on the tube.

Tell me which is the more credible, many times over, with readers/viewers. Why, the second example, of course. Okay, then tell me how anyone can put a dollar value on the difference of the very essence of these two forms of communications, that is, on the disparity in the degrees of *CREDIBILITY?*

To measure the dimensions or effectiveness of a thing, you need a benchmark, a "something" to compare it to. Is a palace with a thousand bedrooms, each with a bath, bigger and more expensive than my townhouse? Pretty much so; I can compare the two surprisingly easy. Okay, so then to what can publicity be compared? Advertising? We just found out that it cannot. Can we compare publicity to—well—*other publicity?*

To do so, we would have to take each publicity item we have in hand and compare it to another, somehow taking into account the following variables:

— **circulation of the newspaper or number of TV viewers** for Item One compared to Item Two;

— **a definitive measurement** of which readers/viewers saw Item One vs. Item Two;

— **a meaningful measurement** of which people *actually absorbed the message* in Items One and Two;

— **the frame of mind of readers/viewers** when they noted Item One compared to their conditions when they noted Item Two, which could influence their interpretations or acceptance level;

— **the length of Item One vs. that of Item Two**, which could be construed to indicate importance;

— **the impact of emotionally-packed words**, which almost certainly will differ between the two examples;

— **the action spurred by One vs. Two**; and . . . well, you see what I mean.

Even if they were to be printed side-by-side on the same page (*very* unlikely – ever!), they still could not be effectively compared.

If you were a really good publicist and got a hundred press and video clips from your single release, you'd have to spend years, just to get a comparison between One and Two. And when you did, the outcome would still be meaningless.

Another example: Assume you're one of your suppliers, a purveyor of tents, let's say. Through good fortune, you've landed a five-inch publicity story in the business section of a 250,000-circulation newspaper serving your city, and the identical five-inch story in a special events-directed trade publication with a national circulation of 25,000. This story announces that you have developed a revolutionary new tent, better than any other on the market, and that you can rent it at half the cost of like-size tents. Which would almost certainly be more valuable to you in terms of probable rentals, meaning *income*?

Obviously, in this case, the trade publication, going directly to the most targeted "audience," will almost always out-perform the daily newspaper in terms of direct dollar potential. That trade magazine sows seed in fertile soil; the newspaper throws a lot of seed on concrete pads, arid soil and salt marshes.

How, then, can you equally rate those two items? What value can you assign to the trade spot over the newspaper coverage? You can do neither, nor can I . . . and neither can those multi-nationals, no matter how hard they still try.

Ask your sponsors or any others who pressure for the advertising-dollar conversion formula how they want to handle measuring negative publicity. God forbid, but suppose there is a major crisis-calibre event involving that sponsor's tent or stage. And suppose there were allegations of negligence in some manner on the sponsor's part. It could get tons of print and air media coverage. Ask them how they want you to convert *that* coverage into advertising dollar values!

Human communications is entirely nebulous, influenced by a kaleidoscope of constantly changing patterns of influences that shade meanings virtually from moment to moment. I would rather try to assign numerical dimensions to beauty. (Forget the one-to-ten appeal scale; it's just as useless. You say that's a two, I say that's a four, you say that's a ten, I say that's an eight, you say *to-MAY-to*, I say *to-MAH-to*, etc.) Indeed, like "beauty" in Ralph Waldo Emerson's poem[3], publicity is its own excuse for being.

OPPORTUNISTIC PUBLICISTS

Final words on publicity:

One of the greatest compliments a publicist can be given is to be called "opportunistic"—one who seizes *every* reasonably good-potential opportunity and wrings it dry to get every drop of benefit from it. This is called "bird-dogging;" fortunate indeed is the event having a bird-dogger, as ugly as that term might be, as a publicist.

Opportunity retrievers know full well that exposure, regardless of "size" or reach, just might attract the right potential sponsors, competitive-cost suppliers, highly productive volunteers or money-dropping new visitors.

I am the first to admit that this book isn't likely to reach a million readers (well, who knows?), but it is designed for a readership of several thousand eventers, who could be of value to . . . well—*events.* I issued an invitation to sixty-one smaller to mid-level and a few larger events, offering to include fully-credited photos of their activities as thematic, non-judgmental dressings for my book.

Cost to each: free.

Total response: three.

Too few to even begin to fulfill my strategy. That's why you'll find no photo artwork herein. I'm just hoping that I happened to have hit only those without opportunistic publicists.

WHAT IS ADVERTISING?

ADVERTISING is the purchase of time or space in communications media for the purpose of conveying one or more prescribed messages, usually designed to sell, convince, or move to action. Such messages are ordinarily recognizable by distinctive display formats in print media and by commercials on television and radio.

If you're seriously considering an advertising program, you must have or expect to get more money than fills the tills of most U.S. events. Insufficient funds means that, for a large majority, advertising, to any effective degree at all, is simply not an option as a stand-alone, event-borne endeavor. (Some events incorporate it into sponsorship agreements, giving extra value in some manner to those sponsors who advertise the event).

Advertising enjoys two extraordinary strengths not shared by any other marketing endeavor. Those qualities that make it worth pursuing are:

— **TIMING CONTROL.** Placement of print or electronic advertising can be decided virtually precisely by the advertiser, especially when use is planned well ahead of desired moment or day of exposure. Space availability in chosen media is the only possible deflective placement concern. Rarely can publicists precisely specify time-use for their material.

— **MESSAGE CONTENT CONTROL.** Publicity material is entirely at the mercy of editors and rewrite desks; its wording can and most frequently is changed around, subject to substitutions, sometimes twisted, sometimes garbled, etc. That is not the case with advertising. Within broad limits labeled good taste, advertising policy and "in the public interest," advertisers are pretty unencumbered when it comes to word selections for their messages. Of course, the more words, the more the cost, so dollars are, in fact, a factor.

Listed below are suggestions that might get the advertising job done at affordable (or no) costs.

Should your event be financially able to field its own ad campaign, try to work with a reputable advertising or marketing agency to plan and carry out your program. Ideally, it would come in as a sponsor, providing services without professional fees, which are a predetermined sum or are about 15% of time or space billings.

For various reasons if you find that such an arrangement is not possible, work directly with the best media, who generally will provide help in the preparation of your print, TV or radio ads.

PSA'S—MIXTURE OF ADVERTISING AND PUBLICITY

If you're event is nonprofit, avidly explore possibilities for the use of Public Service Announcements, referred to as "PSA's."

Both electronic and print media are candidates for PSA submittals. Messages that are a cross between advertising and publicity are meant primarily to benefit the public vis-à-vis some activity or cause. Media frequently deem information about a public event as acceptable subjects for PSA's, which look like commercials but are presented by media without cost to submitters.

A few thoughts about those announcements, however:

·   *Don't take PSA opportunities for granted.* Your event does not have a *right* to them; it is a privilege bestowed entirely at the discretion of media.

·   *Timing of your presentation is, again, a media decision.* Your PSA's might be presented at 4 o'clock every Sunday morning. You are free to attempt time negotiation with the medium, but, in the end, you must take what they give you.

—   *Competition for PSA time and space is fierce.* Your chances for use are improved if you work with the media well in advance of the best-use period, providing your PSA's are of the highest quality. In many cases, you do have to prepare that material, although at times, recipient stations and print outlets will help out with preparation and production.

—   *Many eventers do not know that lots of print media often accept PSA's,* thinking only of radio and television availabilities.

TEAM RADIO

One excellent way to add the advertising advantage to your event, especially if it's in the larger public category, is to entice news media to come aboard as sponsors. As such, they print event ads or carry commercial schedules benefiting your entire happening at little or no cost to the event. They nearly always present generous amounts of featured material and news items as well, since maximizing volume of event mention, tied to their own sponsorship, benefits them. And you.

Radio stations can be especially viable as sponsors, often doing event on-site broadcasting just before and during the event run. On-site or not (and depending on the sponsorship agreement) as sponsors, their very valuable contributions can be a mixed parade of prepared thirty- (:30) or sixty- (:60) second commercials, along with less formalized "promo" plugs, usually of about fifteen seconds' (:15) duration.

[4]Radio, I have found repeatedly, is a long underrated advertising, publicity and promotional tool. Many of my most successful event-advocacy campaigns have been through primary or, surprisingly often, sole use of radio.

Listenership ratios are remarkably high and continue to enjoy steady growth in most markets. During morning and afternoon rush hours (radio's prime times) millions of motorists are strapped-in, often gridlocked message-receivers with radio as their only option for companionship, information or entertainment. And even during the heart of the day, at-home, office and car listeners are surprisingly abundant.

For general-appeal events, adults between twenty-five and forty-nine years of age, with average or a bit higher incomes, and with a couple of kids, will likely be your target group. That being the case, resist the temptation to go after your own favorite rap or classical music station. Following is information that may help you make a more effective selection.

Every station has a "format" or "profile," meaning the type of programming it specializes in or airs exclusively. Its category also indicates which segment(s) of the public seek that kind of programming. Major formats are pretty well described by commonly-used industry terms and symbols, such as:

Talk (T)	News (N)	Sports (S)	Full Service (FS)
Country (C)	Middle-of-Road (MOR)	Adult-Oriented Rock (AOR)	Religious (REL)
Classical (CL)	Ethnic (B-Black; HS-Hispanic)	Easy Listening (EZ)	Contemporary Hit Radio (CHR)
Jazz/New Adult Contemporary (J)		Oldies (circa 1955 and later) (O)	Soft Adult Contemporary (SAC)
Standards (big bands, nostalgia) (ST)			

TEAM TELEVISION

Local television stations (commercial and sometimes cable) can become exceptionally valuable sponsors. Like radio, many actually set up broadcast facilities on event sites, which is a gigantic motivational force for attracting participants to the event. (And incidentally, it shines up sales efforts for attracting non-media sponsors.) This arrangement is usually reserved for the larger, pretty well-established happenings.

But smaller ones can still benefit greatly from TV sponsorship coming only from studio origins. Stations carry event timetables, features on entertainment, news-segment interviews, etc., usually just before or during an event.

TEAM NEWSPAPERS AND MAGAZINES

Print media make equally great sponsors. Many set up on-site information centers or provide some other public service(s) that logically relate to their communications missions. Again, this approach is generally limited primarily to larger public happenings.

Newspapers and magazines, as part of their sponsorship packages, might prepare, produce and distribute (usually free to recipients) special inserts dealing with your event. Those extremely valuable pieces carry event timetables, feature stories, visitor information, sponsor credits and other promotional material.

These same media may also be responsible for the production of souvenir programs sold before and during your event. Characterized frequently by a smart, slick appearance and almost always in color, souvenir programs carry purchased ads from local merchants, sponsors and professional groups, which, coupled with program sales, can often mean its production is paid for, possibly with a profit left over.

Whether print-media sponsors produce either type of publication, they nearly always expand the value of each sponsorship dollar by carrying news and feature material in their regular formats.

EXCLUSIVE MEDIA SPONSORSHIPS?

Shouting matches frequently develop among eventers when this question arises.

Those favoring exclusive media sponsorships contend that:

— Events get better coverage and more of it in sponsoring media.

— Incomes may sometimes be higher when media are granted exclusivity, because events can affix a bigger price tag.

Anti-exclusivity activists declare:

— In the overall, there is *not* more coverage because non-sponsoring media will not support events supported by their competitors.

— Allowing competing media in as sponsors obviously means *more* income.

This will be the only instance in this book that I'll cop-out on the reader. I believe each case must be determined on the individual factors surrounding the subject event. In some markets media grids are such that exclusivity works very well, whereas in others the non-exclusivity strategy works just as well.

> **My only input: GOOD LUCK!**

WHAT ARE PROMOTIONS?

> **PROMOTIONS** include various techniques aimed at attracting attention to an entity and creating or intensifying a desire for it to be purchased or accepted. Very frequently this goal is achieved through incentives, such as contests with prizes, premium offers, coupons and added-value purchases.

As much as any other marketing arm, promotion thrives on creativity. And again, working with a sponsor can be especially rewarding, both to that sponsor and to its event partner.

Sampling and Couponing

These are two related and formidable promotional vehicles—and recognition of their marketing importance is growing speedily by the day. Nothing sells quite so well as having the potential purchaser taste, smell, feel or own free a small version of a product.

And where sampling per se won't work, coupons often will, such as with quickly perishing products or those that must be served piping hot. Promise of sampling/couponing at an event can sometimes tip the scales in favor of a company's decision to go with sponsorship dollar investment, especially if the arrangement guarantees product-category exclusivity.

On-Pack/In-Pack Offers

Eventers who try are often astonished at how easily a promotion of this type can be worked up with a local company. Even hometown outlets of humongous chains can operate independently in creating a local promotion.

Promotional opportunities can be carried on the outside of milk cartons, packages, bottles, cans or wrappers (including such "wrappings" as plastic slip-ons protecting dry-cleaning). For other products, stuffing a printed offer inside its container works just as well. Examples of these promotions for events are:

— Redemption coupons for cents-off or entirely free admission

— Reduced prices of event merchandise, food or beverages

— Raffle tickets (check your lottery laws first or you could end up getting the wrong kind of publicity for your event)

— Redemption tickets for preferred seating or parking or other special treatments, etc.

Radio Promotions

Much of the information presented under Team Radio above applies to this section, so it might be well to review that section before moving on.

Contests that fit radio's characteristic can be especially effective. And many are quite simple. Examples:

— Caller number (blank) gets free passes, merchandise, etc.

— Listeners are invited to prepare and enter favorite dishes using a sponsor's ingredient(s) in a special big-prize competition at the event site.

— Listeners send in post cards nominating some special person to be recognized in some manner at the event. Selection is made during an on-air drawing.

One of my favorite recommendations calls for use of the common phone answering machine. I've suggested that listeners be invited to re-record their answering messages to have them become promotional plugs for the event. ("Hi, Tina and Jeff are getting ready for the big XYZ Event. Don't forget it; it starts next Tuesday. Why don't you meet us there?")

During announced hours, the radio station calls those machines as okayed by listeners who've sent in cards giving permission and promising not to answer during judging hours. A panel of judges (perhaps popular on-air personalities) are listening in the studio. They vote on the three best, most original messages.

Radio promotions nearly always require the purchase of a schedule of commercials to support that promotion. Perhaps sponsorship arrangements with the station could include such a schedule without cost to the event.

Newspaper Media Promotions

Another favorite recommendation of mine calls for the paper to invite readers to redesign fax covering pages.

Immediately prior to the event, a panel of celebrity judges, graphic artists, etc. select fax-covering-page winners in such categories as Most Original, Most Humorous, Most Beautiful, Cutest, and Ugliest. Highly effective as a last-minute promo, winners (and perhaps honorable mentions) would be published in the newspaper. Originals, comprising a continuing promotion, can be put on display in a department store window, busy bank lobby, airport terminal, etc.

That's just one example of print media promotions. Others are event-themed coloring contests, essay competitions, event merchandise sales, word games, hidden objects which, when found, mean big prizes for the finders, and price reductions on general merchandise when shoppers display a lapel button or other identified item.

MARKETING'S "WOMBS"

If you were to take all of the above-described marketing parts and make them work efficiently and effectively in tandem as a miracle machine, that wonderful mechanism could not do the job that one simple jaw-powered tool can do, and that is:

The Word of Mouth Benefit— WOMB (+)

Aunt Martha tells Cousin Bill that Capitol City's huge Summer Fest is the best, most enjoyable thing to come along since the invention of smiles. Bill is almost certainly going to pay closer attention and accept her opinion as more valid more quickly than he will if the same message comes from virtually any other non-personal source. Unless of course, she's the family's resident pathological liar.

Bill goes to Summer Fest and finds that Aunt Martha's appraisal is on target. Big mouth that he is, Bill tells several neighbors, a bunch of people at work, his golf buddies, the bar code checker at the supermarket and on and on and on. Its multiplier effect is remarkable: One tells Two who tell Four who tell Eight who tell Sixteen, etc. It works faster than a politician can break promises. And each carries the validity blessing nearly always inherent in a personally delivered remark from a known personal source.

Conversely, there's:

The Word of Mouth Blast— WOMB (-)

Unfortunately Aunt Martha's strong verbal condemnation of anything, certainly including events, carries just a bit more weight than her compliments. It's a rather widespread human frailty that causes most of us to be just a skosh more attentive to criticism than to praise. This common appeal-of-the-negative is symbolized very well by Alice Roosevelt Longworth's famous embroidered pillow message: "If you can't say anything good about someone, sit right here by me."

Obviously either WOMB is more powerful for *existing* events, where firsthand experience spices up the validity of opinions. However, well marketed *good* plans for a prenatal event gets pretty good personal mouthings—("I hear it's going to be great," "I saw plans on the news last night and it looks cool.")

It's surprising how quickly one or the other comes into play within a very short period after an event's Day One. Can you mold WOMB(+)? Not the way you might want to. Some rather expensive forays into the field of WOMB(+) manipulation have been embarrassing failures. Experimenters have tried paying people to mingle with crowds at bus stops, in movie lines, bars, hair-work places—anywhere—to plant a mouth-transmitted message. If there were successes, they were not well known and apparently were not effective enough to become a broadly used marketing practice. Big reason: people take messages more seriously and quickly from those whom they know personally and whose opinions they value much more so (if at all) than from a talkative stranger at a bus-stop.

About the only way you can engineer either WOMB is through the nature of your event. A good one, of course, gets the (+). WOMB(-), however and very unfortunately, is more easily acquired—and *very, very* difficult to convert to plus status.

That fact results in another reason for the primary motivation behind this book:

> **To promote the paramount need for QUALITY from the inception of any event and the constant, perpetual IMPROVEMENT of that quality.**

In special events, "don't ask, don't tell" doesn't work, either. You don't even have to ask about the quality or success of your event; people will quite often tell you *exactly—and bluntly—*what they think anyway. Unless they're shamed into silence or lies because you're a charity function or a really nice person and a hard worker.

The "How-Dare-You" Celebration

TORNADO GARDENS MOBILE HOME PARK OPENS IN KANSAS

VERY HYPOTHETICAL CASE STUDY AND ITS USES

Throwing caution to the wind, so to speak, Dare-Dot-Com

Development Corp. has built the huge, maxi-lavish

Tornado Gardens Mobile Home Park Estates near

Wichita, Kansas. This project, the largest, most costly

of its genre in the entire world, is now the flagship

of the 104 parks in the D-D-C chain.

Being the consummate marketer, after much re-

search, D-D-C firmly believes Kansas is one of

three or four Midwestern states destined to become

economic, cultural and social forces in the first

two or so decades of the 21st Century. That's

why the company has invested tons of money in

that state, tornadoes or not.

Capitalizing on the project name, which flies in the face of its location (one of the nation's most frequently traveled twister trails), D-D-C expects to attract lots of national media attention. . . and, not coincidentally, also to capture literally thousands of lessees and buyers for its ToGaMoHo Estates sites. To help things along, the company has assigned its Marketing and Public Relations Departments to come up with a huge $3 million grand opening festival — one possibly becoming an annual big-bucks profit center for the development company.

As the conclusion of this chapter on Marketing, I have prepared material related to this hypothetical case study. These documents are meant to serve as models for similar items you will be creating for your RFP response.

NOTE: At the bottom of each first page of the following documents, you will find my "fun contact identity." In your "real" versions, you will want to replace it with phone numbers, and/or fax numbers and/or E-Mail addresses—whichever is/are best for quick media contacts.

Opening Fact Sheet

Grand Opening Celebration May 1-5

TORNADO GARDENS MOBILE HOME PARK OPENS IN KANSAS

THEME: *Reflecting the daring decision to name a Kansas mobile home park Tornado Gardens, high-pressure opening ceremonies feature performers who (1) risk life and limb to entertain, and/or (2) who are characterized by speed, fast-paced action or other movements reminiscent of tornadoes. May was chosen because it attracts more tornadoes than any other month.*

Parade of Those Who Dare to Dare
(May 1; Depart 7 p.m.)

Daredevil drivers in their "unique" vehicles take VIP's and media from Wichita hotels to a specially built station at Tornado Gardens.

The *Darena*

This temporary amphitheater comfortably seats the 5,000 special guests (May 1 only), with bleachers for 10,000 general-public guests, on that opening night. All 15,000 seats are available the remaining four nights for the public-at-large.

Darena Spectacular
(7:30-10:00 p.m.)

WARM-UP—The Would-WINDS, playing the top 40s, start off the event that is fast-paced, non-stop. There are no breaks until completion of the Grand Finale.

FANFARE AND OVERTURE—The 60-piece Cyclone Symphony Orchestra plays all music for the show.

THOUSAND AND ONE TWISTERS—1,000 dancers, acrobats, jugglers, twirlers, cape artists, etc., create a production number covering the entire arena floor.

FALL OF THE FIRE-A-CHUTES—200 sky-divers from 20 planes drop into *Darena*, each carrying a torch. With the Twisters, they form a parade that leads in...

CONTACT: Bob Jackson   1-800-555-555   FAX 1-800-555-5556

THE RECKLESS WRECKERS—138 vehicles of many descriptions jump over each other, crash together, over-turn and even burn while being driven

GRAND FINALE—all participants jam the field, creating a giant whirling pinwheel of action, color and light. Twenty giant helicopters hover overhead, stirring up tornadic winds that, with a sky full of fireworks surrounding the arena, bring the spectacle to a loud, action-packed close.

Twist and Shout Supper Dancing
(10:00 p.m.- 2:00 a.m.)

Opening night special guests enjoy dancing to five musical groups, each playing styles of music from different eras. Each is located on a different outdoor stage.

Darena Dancing
(10:00 p.m.-2:00 a.m.)

Members of the general public dance on the arena floor following the show, until 2:00 a.m. Music is provided by three groups, each in different area if the stadium. Free refreshments are served.

Show and Dancing
(May 2-5; 7:30 p.m.- 2:00 a.m.)

Full shows and dancing are offered the following four nights for the public. No VIP arrangements are scheduled after May 1.

Free Tickets

Tickets are required for public seating all five nights. They are available (limit: six per family) at special promotional kiosks in downtown Wichita and all local malls. Seating is on a first-come, first-served basis.

D.A.R.E. Benefit

Collections are being taken all five nights, proceeds going to law enforcement's popular drug-fighting program. Goal is $100,000.

Total Number of Event Personnel

4,789 artists actually participate in the arena show. 766 specialized backstage personnel assist performers. 271 auxiliary assistants are on hand throughout the park.

Size of Darena

Its "floor" is equivalent to 1.5 football fields

Five-Day Cost

Entire production costs total $3 million

General Fact Sheet

PARK COST: $562 MILLION   SIZE: 13,712 ACRES

TORNADO GARDENS MOBILE HOME PARK OPENS IN KANSAS

Name

"Tornado Gardens Mobile Home Park Estates," chosen to appeal to under-50, somewhat adventurous, affluent adults for whom the project was specifically designed.

Park Concept

Combines attributes mandated by those wanting year-round or seasonal get-away, upscale homes in choice, maximum-security locations; saturated in snob appeal.

Squall Mall

Project centerpiece; collection of 70 boutiques, service outlets, fitness centers, auto catalog store and shooting ranges; available: designer attire, gourmet cuisine (Turkey take-out—the nation, not the bird; Funnel Cake Drive-Thru), spas for the fat and emaciated, mail-order Italian sports cars, jet aircraft showrooms, and jewelers having nothing lower priced than $5,000 trinkets.

Lightning Golf and Country Club

18-hole championship course, designed by seven of the world's top golfers; all hats and carts required to be equipped with lightning rods; Country Club House features four ballrooms, each accommodating 1,000-4,000 guests.

Wind Shear Intercontinental Jetport

Accommodates 747 and smaller; parking for 475 private jets; full-service facility, including U.S. Customs pass-through and expedient, non-quarantine pet clearance unit.

Home Sites

1,278 in number, each measuring one-half acre to ten acres; all with mandatory indoor-outdoor pools; cost range: $300,000 to $1 million.

Home Designs

Various modifications of French Chateau and Maison styles, all featuring mansard roofs, terraces; no two look-a-likes; 4-6-car garages; apartments for 6-10 domestic employees; 7-16 bedrooms and like-number baths; 2-4 food preparation areas; main dining rooms for 12-48 guests; cost range: $750,000 to $4 million.

Monthly Fee

Association fee for common area maintenance and other services and privileges: $5,300 monthly

CONTACT: Bob Jackson   1-800-555-555   FAX 1-800-555-5556

Thoroughfares	Main Gate No. 1 Entrance: Yellow Brick Road; Gate No. 2: Dorothy Boulevard; Gate No. 3 Toto Avenue; Others: Scarecrow Place; Auntie Em Street, Wizard Way.
Underground Shelters	Four subterranean weather shelters, said to accommodate total of 8,155 inhabitants for up to three days in full comfort.
Medical Facilities	Headquartered full-time in underground shelters; 100-bed hospital; six full-time physicians; total medical staff of 23, including three psychiatrist, one specializing in agoraphobia.
Project Size	13,712 acres, one-half size of Walt Disney World.
Project Cost	Total: $562 million, not including homes.
Population	Maximum: 6,000-8,000 est.
Staff	Full-time: 319; part-time and seasonal: additional 187
Developer	Dare-Dot-Com Development Corp, New York, New York.

MEDIA RELEASE

$3 MILLION PARTY FOR 75,000

TORNADO GARDENS MOBILE HOME PARK OPENS IN KANSAS

FOR RELEASE UPON RECEIPT:

Throwing caution to the wind, so to speak, developers have chosen May, the month when twisters hit most often, to stage a very special event to open their half-billion-dollar Tornado Gardens Mobile Home Park Estates.

And it's located smack in the middle of Kansas' cyclone expressway.

Easily the costliest and largest (13,712 acres) of its kind in the world, Tornado Gardens has been designed to appeal to those who would tempt Fate by booking first-class passage aboard the *Andrea Doria II, Lusitania II* or even *Titanic II*, should such ever exist.

Thirteen black cats walking under ladders in front of broken mirrors mean absolutely nothing to those in line to buy the $300,000 to $1 million *sites* on which to place *manufactured homes,* each in the affluent neighborhood of $750,000 to $4 million. Homes? Read that palaces (mandatory: indoor-outdoor swimming pools).

Spending $3 million for a kick-off bash, developer Dare-Dot-Com is producing a four-evening repeat spectacular for 75,000, calling for the talents of 4,789 performers.

With "The Big Twister Dare" as its theme, this event is anchored by the 60-piece, especially-created Cyclone Symphony, which plays periodically throughout the non-stop spectacular. Action contin-

CONTACT: Bob Jackson   1-800-555-555   FAX 1-800-555-5556

---

ues with "1001 Twisters," composed of dancers, acrobats, jugglers, twirlers and so on, is a massive production number.

Fall of the Fire-a-Chutes followed by the demolition wars of "The Reckless Wreckers" blows the show literally into a whirlwind finale crowned by 20 giant helicopters amidst fireworks surrounding the specially-built stadium.

Called "Darena," (Dare-arena) is the size of one and a half football fields, and it seats 15,000 special guests and members of the public.

Those honored guests include 5,000 leaders of government, industry, entertainment and potential site-home buyers. Those 479 who have already made their purchases are being given special attention all five nights.

As might be expected, law enforcement's D.A.R.E. drug-fighting program benefits from nightly hat-passings. Goal is $100,000.

Tornado Gardens' amenities include its own "downtown," called Squall Mall, which offers pricey boutiques, service outlets, fitness centers and even an auto catalogue where guests may order the Mercedes of their choice. Jet aircraft showrooms and minimum-purchase ($5000) jewelry stores are other enticements.

Lightning Golf and Country Club vies for attention with Wind Shear Intercontinental Jetport (special pet pass-through is promised). "Just in case," Tornado Gardens has its own 8,000-plus-capacity underground cluster of disaster shelters, one of which also houses its 100-bed, full-service hospital.

MEDIA ADVISORY

GRAND OPENING CELEBRATION MAY 1-5

TORNADO GARDENS MOBILE HOME PARK OPENS IN KANSAS

MEDIA ADVISORY **APRIL 17**

SPECIAL MEDIA ARRANGEMENTS FOR OPENING DAY, *MAY 1*:

√ 9:00 a.m. — Media reception and Administration area tour

and Squall Mall, Medical Center, Underground Shelters

√ 11:00 a.m. — Combined brunch and media conference

√ 12:30 p.m. — Tours in limousines of Lightening Golf Course,

Wind Shear Airport, Model Homes

√ 5:00 p.m. — Return media to hotels, food trays in rooms

√ 6:45 p.m. — Media Limos depart to participate in Parade

√ 7:30 p.m. — Opening Spectacular at Darena, special seating

√ 10:00 p.m. — Twist(er) and Shout Supper Dancing

√ 2:00 a.m. — (or earlier) Media limos shuttle to hotels

MEDIA HEADQUARTERS: Tempest Ballroom, Country Club

MEDIA HOT LINES: 1-800-CYCLONE

1-800-TWISTER

CONTACT: Bob Jackson **1-800-555-555** **FAX 1-800-555-5556**

Notes

[1]For additional material on event marketing, see *SE:IO*, Introduction and Chapter 6

[2]For other information on this important subject, especially on print media publicity, refer to *SE:II*, Chapter 6, pp. 53-58

[3]"Rhodora! if the sages ask thee why

This charm is wasted on the earth and sky,

Tell them, dear, that if eyes were made for seeing,

Then Beauty is its own excuse for being." *The Rhodora*

[4]If you have station choices, do your homework to assure best selection of that/those coming closest to fitting the demographic profiles you most want to reach. For advertising, publicity and/or promotional strategies, I strongly recommend these two excellent complementary sources:

American Radio, published twice annually by Duncan's American Radio, Inc., P.O. Box 90284, Indianapolis, IN 46290; phones: 847.577.4660 or 317.844.0988. An indispensable source for pinpointing demographic reaches (examples: adults 18-49, men 18-24, women 25-54, etc.) Also rates stations by popularity (Arbitron audience counts) in the top 200-plus U.S. markets, which, surprisingly, includes some very small population centers.

Bacon's Radio Directory, published annually by Bacon's Information, Inc., 332 So. Michigan Ave., Chicago, IL 60604; phone: 312-922-2400; usually available in larger libraries. One of the best directories for radio stations, networks, syndicates, programs by titles and topics and national call-letter index. Most important: it provides radio station addresses, phone and fax numbers, formats, summarized targeted audiences and names with titles of station contacts.

Bacon's also publishes several other excellent media directories, among them one for daily and weekly newspapers, print media syndicates and wire services; another for magazines; and a third for commercial and cable television stations, syndicates and networks. Databases are also available.

Chapter Five

AEROBICS FOR EVENT HEARTS

Events are more and more exploring and finding ways to serve their communities or specialized constituencies other than providing only entertainment, a place to overeat or simply something "to do that's different." Below is a compendium of ways I've come across in my years of studying events, along with a few suggestions of my own, that might be worth trying by those wanting more "heart" in their events.

This exercise does wonders for everybody's heart; yours, your staff's and volunteers'. Your PR index, your present or future event and those public(s) you serve now or later will all be better for it.

FOR ENFORCED ABSENTEES

In every community there are people who are unable to participate in events as much as they might like to. Smart and thoughtful eventers are taking some of their programming to those who can't join the crowds on site.

Many acts are booked with the provision that they will be available during a given day-and-time frame to go to centers for enforced absentees. Among them:

hospitals	day-care centers
retirement communities	care-givers for seniors
hospices	mental retardation facilities

As logic dictates, check with administrators of these destinations before booking talent appearances. Timing is important, of course, but also determine the following:

— types of entertainment permitted and those strictly prohibited

— dimensions of spaces allotted for performers

— indoor or outdoor venue

— availability of changing rooms

— arrangements for stowage and protection of personal items, equipment and props

— recommendations on degrees and nature of performer interaction with audience members

— restrictions on animal participation

— policies on electrified amplification

— parking for casts' cars, equipment trucks, etc.

— youngsters' fears of large costumed characters

— policies regarding media coverage of performer visits

Picking up on the latter point, media often love to cover such visits, particularly those to children's hospitals or wards. Some eventers fear accusations of exploitation, but this should not be of concern. Pleasure given to the indigent far, far outweighs the possibilities of such grumbling from negative thinkers. (I have arranged these visits for many years and have heard that allegation not more than two or three times, which I summarily ignored—until I recalled them just now.)

Acts that work especially well in such venues are:

— small musical ensembles

— self-accompanied singers

— guitarists, banjo players, fiddlers

— dancers (controlled swinging, please)

— animals (not wild, house-broken)

— jugglers

— sword/fire-swallowers (not too appropriate near oxygen tanks nor children's wards, youngsters might try it at home)

— basketball manipulators

— pantomime artists

— magicians (particularly popular; however, avoid sawing people in half where patients are awaiting surgery)

— balloon sculptors

— corporate or sports costumed mascots (caution: some children freak out when a nightmare-size rabbit or Santa Claus looms in their hospital room doorways)

— costumed holiday characters—Santa, Easter Bunny, elves

— costumed storybook characters – Horner, Jack; Mary & Lamb

— ventriloquists

— storytellers

— unicyclists (good in orthopedics, "just in case")

Related to the above, but not in the heart-tug category, is taking "parts" of your event to popular off-site gathering spots, such as downtown plazas or parks where workers take their lunches, malls, commuter debarkation points, etc. during the run of the event. These appearances can be great marketing devices by giving potential attendees a sample of your entertainment lineup. Don't forget to banner (event and perhaps sponsors) and do notify media.

ON-SITE, FOR SPECIAL GUESTS

PROVIDE SIGN LANGUAGE COMMUNICATORS FOR THE HEARING IMPAIRED.

Volunteers can usually be found to provide this important service. Even if there are no audience members with hearing difficulties, signer presence reminds people of the need to support programs for the deaf.

GO BEYOND THE LAW IN ACCOMMODATIONS FOR THE PHYSICALLY CHALLENGED.

There are laws which must be observed for facilitating visitors in wheelchairs, but do more than those regulations require, such as the following:

— Roping off or otherwise reserving sections in audience areas

— Booking talented, encumbered performers

— Preparing stages and other performing areas to meet their needs

SPECIAL ON-SITE ARRANGEMENTS FOR THE HOMELESS, BATTERED WIVES, ABUSED CHILDREN, MAKE-A-WISH FOUNDATION YOUNGSTERS, ETC.

Sometimes a simple phoned invitation to these groups is sufficient. Many can send their own staff members or volunteers to be with those who should be accompanied. But an especially hearty gesture is to have your own *very carefully selected and trained* volunteers serving as on-site hosts for these special visitors, even when they're accompanied by their own people. Hosting volunteers should be those with especially mega-size hearts, big capacities for kindness, and the patience of obsessive lottery players.

> **BIG CAUTION**: In virtually every case, the last thing you want to do is to magnetize any kind of attention on these special guests, on-site or through media. *Before* Event Day One, you should announce to news outlets your plans for welcoming those in these categories. Once that announcement is made, stifle any further media attention during your event. If administrators of those groups want such coverage, they should be entirely responsible for media contacts and conduct. Your publicity volunteers should be aware of all such arrangements and should offer to be of help.

YOUR CONSTITUENCY'S MOST HONORED HONOREES

I'm going to run into flak when I suggest this, but here goes anyway. Slowly but surely, beauty contests are on their way out. That's right, o-u-t. And strictly as an event consultant, I'm glad.

One of the most desirable products of the feminist movement has been to declare these throw-backs sexist and to press for their abolition. I wish them every success. In place of letting high cheekbones, low body weight and birthdays determine event "royalty," why not make your event *really* meaningful by having truly deserving people – those who have made remarkable and substantial contributions to the community, profession, arts, sports, etc. — be "crowned" and heavily honored?

A fireman who has saved lives, foster parents who have successfully cared for scores of children, a particularly effective school teacher – these and others like them should be the honored "court." They should be given preferred seating, rides in parades, medals, distinctive attire, etc. They are the ones who have *earned* the right to be honored "royalty."

SUNDAY MORNINGS

Perhaps jockeying for the most favorable positioning in The Hereafter, *and* because I truly believe it's good eventsership, I recommend this strategy for happenings that straddle Sundays, when there is a natural fit:

- **DO NOT SCHEDULE "REGULAR" EVENT ELEMENTS BEFORE 11 A.M.**

INSTEAD

- **LET RELIGIONS BE PART OF YOUR EVENT WITH RELATED SERVICES**

At the very start of your event-planning period, publicly call for an assembly of representatives from all religious organizations. Tell them that you will not interfere with Sunday worship by extending your regular activities into their usual regular service hours. Tell them, however, that you wish to make them an integral part of your event by suggesting that they conduct lighter, fun services that are in some way related to it. Examples:

For patriotic motifs—churches decorate in red, white and blue, with themed sermons or homilies on the greatness of this nation, music reflecting gratitude for our nation's many blessings and prayers asking for continued help and protection.

For sports and athletic events—theme services to emphasize the importance of healthy competition, the permanent need for fairness in games and lives, winning by striving, etc.

For food themes—services pivot on giving thanks for our abundance, collecting food for the needy that morning, enjoying services over a potluck or ticketed breakfast as sites for the actual services, etc.

IF APPROPRIATE, CONDUCT YOUR OWN ECUMENICAL SERVICES[1]

Set aside one hour on Sunday morning to offer a non-denominational service on-site, preferably on your main stage or in a large open area with platforms. This very special occasion, timed to avoid the most popular "church hours," 9-11 a.m., can take several forms, among them:

Sunrise Commemorative Service—honoring those who have died for public benefit—armed forces personnel, law enforcement officers, firefighters, etc.

Services Asking Special Blessings (11-12 a.m.)—for athletic competitors, those who serve and protect, your volunteers, our nation, victims of a recent disasters, etc.

Simple Ecumenical Services (11-12 a.m.)—unthemed, giving those who prefer an opportunity to participate in non-denominational worship. This can be especially welcome to tourists who, of course, have no church affiliations in your community.

Sunday Morning Brunch—capitalizing on what has become virtually a family institution. Ask your food and beverage supporters and suppliers if they can see value to offering a brunch-of-fare, say from 11 a.m. until 1 or 2 p.m.

CAUTIONS ON CAUSE MARKETING

This section relates primarily to the establishment of new, usually one-time-only events, put on primarily to raise funds for some designated recipient(s). However, its cautions hold for continuing, sequential events that may be approached to have a fund-raising cause attached to them, either on a once-only basis or as a permanent adjunct.

By their very circumstances (generally attracting people with money, surrounding them in favorable circumstances) special events are great vehicles for fund-raising. In nearly every case, this effort is entirely commendable and honest. But in some, it's neither.

Many states and cities have very specific ordinances designed to protect the public from cause charlatans. Before you structure a fund-raising event, check with local authorities to assure that all parties are in full compliance with those regulations.

If you're approached by event producers, organizers or managers, asking your event to participate in fund-raising or seeking you to put on an ad hoc charity event, before you agree, find the answers to these two important questions:

Question 1: What percentage of funds will go directly to the benefiting charity and what percentage will be consumed in event production, management and broker fees and expenses?

"Good" and "bad" percentages can vary according to unique circumstances enveloping each program. However, if you find that less than 75% of all proceeds will go to *specified* beneficiaries, be doubly careful about entering into such agreement. Find out to your complete satisfaction before signing why a larger percentage is not earmarked for the beneficiary.

Question 2: What is the actual cost in dollars of event production and management?

If, for example, the estimated cost of the event is put at $100,000, and indications are given that it will cost $50,000 for its operations, really check it out. Find out why. It may be worth it, it may not.

If you're not absolutely sure, safe strategy is to take *the contract and a line-item, fully detailed budget of fees and expenses* to a qualified lawyer, your state or local charity-governing unit; the Better Business Bureau (if applicable); your state attorney general's office, city or district attorney, and knowledgeable business people whose opinions you especially respect.

If you're recruited by those who have staged this same type of event previously in other markets, ask for at least three references – names, addresses and phone numbers of best sources, which ideally will be those in charge of official accounting for their events.

If they have worked it before in only one or two markets, treat this opportunity as if it's a first-timer. If they unduly delay or refuse *for any reason* to supply reference information, bid them farewell, unless you get exceptionally favorable responses from those sources suggested above.

When you get reference information, immediately make contacts, asking each these important questions (perfect world: they'll provide you written, certified responses):

A. How many times did you work with these people?

B. What was the bottom-line financial result each time?

C. How did final income figure(s) compare with their projections?

D. What was the *actual* attendance at each?

E. Each time, how did total attendance compare with projections?

    (Ask for an explanation if there is a sizable disparity.)

F. How would you term your working relationship with these people?

G. How do you feel your community or constituency reacted to the event?

H. Would you work again with these people? If not, why not?

Fortunately, over the years, special eventers have formed what is today a tight-knit community, eagerly willing to help each other. As such, in most cases, you can expect eager participation in this kind of survey, with honest and complete responses. Once you have this information in hand, combine it with the results of the first two questions. That should give you a pretty solid idea of the direction you should take.

For a section on having a big heart, this subject may seem a bit brittle. But, in this matter, it's better to be hard-hearted than brokenhearted.

HAVING A GOOD NEIGHBOR'S HEART

Your event may occupy its site(s) for only a few days each year, but those can be long and tortured days for neighbors when your event isn't considerate of them. There are instances when events had to move—and a few which simply went out of business—as a result of neighbors' complaints. Here are some suggestions to help assure that your event has a very good neighbor's heart:

— As soon as your event plans are made for its next edition, **call a meeting of those living *and working* within several blocks' radius of your site.** Make it a social event that's full of pretty detailed (but valid and *interesting)* information—what your plans are, who'll be name entertainers, days and hours of operation, etc. Emphasize what you're doing to keep your event from intruding on or otherwise negatively impacting their lives. Most important, *give them a full opportunity to be heard*, letting them present actual or perceived problems or fears, and promise that *within reason* you will look into solving those issues. (Promise no more than that; an event is going to cause *some* discomfort to some one some time, so you cannot and should not promise to end all problems.)

— With adequate signage supported by periodic volunteer or police patrols, **keep event-goers from blocking nearby driveways and parking spaces**. This one problem can transform even the most ordinarily tranquil people into fire-breathing haridans and cauldron-stirring warlocks, spewing venomous words even they can't define.

— **Aim sound systems away from residential areas or businesses during their operational hours**. If this doesn't entirely solve the decibel problem, try to employ sound baffling, either specifically designed devices, such as framed sheets of canvass, vinyl or plywood. When laying out multi-tent-quartered happenings, try to place tents in configurations that enable them to double as sound-absorbers. Also, expanses of parked automobiles can help, as can fortunately-placed trees, which you should use to best sound advantage (see Chapter Three).

— **Regularly police the neighborhood to pick up any trash** carelessly discarded by event-goers. This simple thoughtfulness will make many friends for your event.

— No matter how well you prepare your community, however, there are likely to be some activities that will disturb some parts of it . . . further proof of the inability of please all the people all the time. Closing down thoroughfares for parades, foot or wheeled races, use by emergency vehicles or special parking—even for a comparatively short time—may whip some residents into the quick-rip, high-spin cycle. **Try to avoid or minimize these interruptions through creative problem solving.**

— On a broader scale, **take every step to assure an environment-friendly event.** And don't just give this need lip service. Specifically plan recycling of paper, glass and plastics. Disturb natural growth as little as possible, *and be sure to return your site to its pre-use (or better) ecological condition* immediately after your event. These actions assure your event's recognition as a good *world* neighbor, present and future.

MERCHANTS OF MENACE: INVITATIONS TO TERROR

By their very nature and missions, special events make up the primary industry for bringing together large groups of people. That's our whole reason for being; People—crowds of 'em—are our business.

Unfortunately, People—large, medium or small crowds of them—are also the business of demented, evil, reason-vacant minds . . . those who feel their opinions, doctrines, convictions—whatever—must be blown or shot into the world psyche with bombs or bullets in crowds of innocent people. Sometimes it's just for the perverted pleasure of causing trouble, of being noticed, of interrupting life.

This is the stuff of terrorism.

Unfortunately, our people industry provides some of the best opportunities for these Merchants of Menace (my apologies to W. Shakespeare). We saw state-of-the-art terrorism during international games in Munich in 1972, with the mind-numbing slaughter of Israeli athletes and coaches. This segment of this book is being written within hours after the blast that killed one and injured more than a hundred at Centennial Park during the 1996 Atlanta games, despite the maximum, truly valiant efforts of the greatest force of security experts ever assembled for a special event.

But assemblies need not have the huge dimensions of an international athletic quorum to provide terrorists with opportunities. Any crowd will do, including your event's. Therefore, in view of this affliction, which apparently is going to be around for some time, *every* event must have an expertly designed plan to handle such exigencies (see Chapter 4).

No one can completely stop terrorism; that's now a given. But we can minimize the impact of those sick acts, if we know how, when and what to do. No matter how free of worry you may feel, it is imperative that you have in place a fully effective, entirely efficient plan for handling crises. Unfortunately, no crowd, no individual, is safe during this continuing Pain of Terror.

Without arousing fear in your community by making this a big thing media-wise, your security group, along with event staff members and executive volunteers, should meet with local law enforcers and public safety personnel who are specialists in crisis conditions, especially terrorism attacks. Ask them for help that, hopefully, will never be needed, knowing that it's better to have it and not need it than to need it and not have it.

A PLAN FOR ALL REASONS

Equally important: emergencies other than those caused by terrorists must be fully addressed in your total crisis plan, including fire, accidents, personal health emergencies (heart attacks, sun strokes, etc.), weather (very important; consider severe thunder/lightning storms, high winds, flooding, etc.), and such crimes as robbery, assault . . . even murder.

You need experts to help you formulate such a plan. And fortunately, the best experts are almost always available at no cost for their services. Among them are law enforcers and investigators, firefighters, hospital emergency personnel, paramedics, traffic and transportation specialists, governmental tourism promotion offices, representatives from other events already having such plans, and meteorologists.

Here is a suggested agenda for meetings with those experts:

— **Make those specialists entirely knowledgeable about your venue** and provide them with a detailed written description of your event. Good location maps are especially helpful – and be sure to keep them up to date.

— Take experts to the site, walk them through your planned layout, let them get a feel for what will go on, when and where. **Be wide open for their advice in means of protecting life and property**.

— **Give them absolutely current plot plans or schematics of your event layout**; issue new versions to all advisors when there are any significant alterations whatsoever.

— **Provide them with solid estimates of expected numbers** of people to be on site at maximum hours of activities.

— **Get their input on mass communication needs** – public address systems, radios, walkie-talkies, beepers, telephones (open and coin-operated), etc.

— **Together, determine safety measures** for and routes of evacuation procedures, points where evacuees can be safely accommodated. Get their advice on how to announce emergency measures with a maximum of controlled crowd reaction. Too frequently, more casualties result from crowd stampanic than from primary problem sources.

— **Devise a plan for facilitating emergency vehicles** and personnel en route to and within your site(s).

— **Determine which event staff and volunteer personnel should receive special crisis training** – *and be certain that such training is given.* It's wise to hold such instructions at least annually, both for new people and as refreshers for returnees.

— **Find out what fundamental medical supplies and equipment should be a regular part of your event scene,** get them, keep them on hand in fully useable condition, and let every appropriate person know where those items are stowed and how to use them.

— **Have your Marketing/Publicity people as integral parts of this entire procedure**. (See Chapter 4).

These recommendations may seem a bit hyper-dramatic, maybe even somewhat over-reactive, especially if you're involved with a small-town festival. But they are essential; you *must* take these measures prior to every time your event takes place, regardless of its size.

You want your people to have happy hearts. You also want your people to have happy hearts *that keep beating.*

HIGH PRIORITY: MAKE NATURE SECOND NATURE

Events prospering in the next century will have built-in parameters for protection of the environment, plans whose implementation is second nature for those events.

Federal, state and most city governments have environmental protection organizations eager to help you devise such a plan. There are also companies in many regions which can be contracted to handle recycling and other measures satisfying ecological safety needs.

Most providers of portable toilets are also dedicated to environmental safety. Select one that will be fully sensitive to this matter.

Here are some agenda items you might bring to their attention when seeking their advice and assistance:

— What materials found in your event can be recycled? How can you obtain the cooperation of event-goers in separating collectables from other refuse? What is the destination of these discards?

— What familiar event items should be avoided in the interest of environmental protection? (For example, balloons made from certain material can harm wildlife. Which balloons are safe; how should any balloons be used?)

— Don't forget that the atmosphere can also be contaminated by sound, light and odor. What can be done to prevent such intruders?

— If natural growth or animals must be disturbed during preparations for and the run of your event, determine how such disorders can be minimized and what steps should be taken to return your site(s) to pre-use, ecologically-sound condition.

— In vacating your site, determine if there are any reasonable measures you might take to improve its original condition. (Planted flowers might be left, pre-event litter removed, unsightly structures taken away, etc.)

Through advance and during-run publicity, you can notify the public of your plans to protect the environment and solicit their participation by spelling out exactly what they can do during their visits to help with this worthwhile effort. You and they owe it to the world. Everyone must get to the heart of this very important matter.

---

[1]Check with local church authorities to determine whether there are any programs or observances they plan that you might integrate into your services. However, bypass those that are too parochial to work well with what should be non-denominational policies.

Chapter Six

Improving Organizational Set-ups

"Our festival stinks. I really think it's headed for *total* failure, and soon. There doesn't seem to be anything going right. There's so much in-fighting that nothing gets done. I wish I hadn't taken this job. Every minute's just a nightmare. We need help—and lots of it."

Can this festival be saved?

Ms. Desperate was near tears when she spoke those words after cornering me, literally, between sessions at a recent annual meeting of the International Festival and Events Association[1]. I thought coffee might help, so we each filled a cup of the free IFEA brew and sat down opposite each other in an out-of-the-way hotel lobby alcove. After many l-o-n-g minutes of hand-wringing and quivering lips, she had described in painful detail the horrible viruses afflicting her paling, ailing festival.

Let me summarize them for you:

— There are so many committees that administering them is nearly impossible.

— Cooperation between committees has long been buried under "this is our turf."

— Trouble-maker volunteers are major obstacles to . . . well, *everything*.

— Long-time volunteers won't let go of *their* areas, most of which need to be dropped or certainly improved.

— Many self-serving members of its board of directors constantly squabble among themselves, creating gridlocks that would make the government proud.

— This festival is the fifteen-year-old brainchild of the chamber of commerce, which continues to play what Ms. D feels is the role of an abusive parent—plenty of interference and plain old politicking.

— No really significant public-participation offering has been added in at least five years.

— Attendance has been steadily declining, as has sponsor numbers and levels of dollars by those who have remained.

We had just a few minutes to explore solutions, and she was fair with me in her early admission that the festival is in such bad financial shape that they couldn't hire me, even for my usual paltry fee, for an on-site, months-long study needed to find solutions. This event is still in bad shape, from what the surprisingly accurate event grape-net communicates.

So Ms. Desperate, for the pitifully small price of this book, I will try to help you while I'm advising others, since, unfortunately, there are many events that share one or more of these difficulties with you.

Let's take each problem and see what we can do with it.

ORGANIZATIONAL FLAB? OR TOO LEAN AND MEAN?

How many committees do you need? Enough. Okay, how many is enough? Not too many, not too few. If there is a simpler answer that fits all needs, I don't know it.

There are as many different organizational flow charts and operational grids as there are special events. To try to devise one or two or ten to satisfy even one or two or ten operations is an exercise in futility. Here is a plan that may help you and Ms. Desperate determine the most suitable organizational patterns:

Make a list of absolutely indispensable needs, tasks, responsibilities, etc. that must be accommodated just for your event to maintain a threshold-to-function. Ms. Desperate's might read something like this:

administration/supervision[2]	food
marketing	beverages
entertainment	merchandise
transportation	security/safety
maintenance	decorations
sponsorships	finance
human resources	supplies
communications	site preparations

At first consideration, it would appear that she might need sixteen committees to handle all needs. If her event is one that attracts between perhaps 100,000 and 300,000 *actual* visits, this organizational stack might be suitable. However, if her event size is above 500,000 *actual* visits, she will probably have to add several others, which could be taken from the list of committees ending this chapter. But if her event attracts between 35,000 and 100,000, she might increase efficiency by combining fairly similar or strongly interrelated duties, thus reducing committee numbers.

For purposes of illustration, let's assume that our study shows her event can reduce its committee number to six. She might end up with a really efficient grid, something like this:

THESE COMMITTEES . . .	WHOSE DUTIES ARE . . .
administration/supervision	human resources (volunteer or staff), legal, contracts, policy-making
vendor	food, beverages, merchandise, purchase and distribution of supplies
public safety	security, safety, transportation, maintenance, communications
finance	budgeting, expenditures, sponsorships
operations	entertainment, decorations, site preparations, pedestrian traffic flow
marketing	publicity, promotions, advertising media coordination, graphics

Instead of sixteen, Ms. Desperate now has only six committees to get everything done—and for which she will have to recruit volunteers when vacancies develop and serve as supervisor.[3] Depending on the wishes of Chairholders, some or all of these groups could have assistant chairpersons, each responsible for one of the obvious "subdivisions."

Should her event attract fewer than 35,000 *actual* visits, she might need committees only for vendors and operations, depending on the profile or theme of her event (food, sports, music, whatever), all other needs being met by individuals serving within an administrative unit.

ATTEMPTING REORGANIZATION

There are two basic strategies for bringing about organizational improvement through structural realignment. Fact: neither work every time, but they're probably more effective than sloppier methods.

One of the best ways to go about reorganization, especially in committee number reduction that calls protective turfism into play, is to create the suggested framework, kneading it until you are absolutely certain that *every* lump has been worked out. That means having all questions answered about it, then attempting to get board shakers and doers to buy into it. Try sitting down one-on-one and laying out your reasoning.

Very important: *you must have done your homework. All of it!* Have an answer for every conceivable question or possible deflection point. And be sure to make your target feel that he or she is the only worthwhile person on earth, without whose superior skills you could not possibly hope to succeed in getting your reorganization accepted by a board majority.

A second reorganization approach is to form an ad hoc task force to study needs and make recommendations for needed changes. But remember: you take what you get from a group effort; it may not always be just what you want. Your chances of getting a board sanction are somewhat better, since it will likely react more positively to the force of multi-person recommendations than to your single-voice suggestions.

Of course, if you own a spiked velvet glove personality that also wears its imaginary high black boots (*very* soft leather) and wields an invisible-but-don't-forget-it's-there whip, you might enjoy a twin-world resolution. You can get your way while it's endorsed and presented by the task force.

S-L-O-W EXPECTATIONS

Bear in mind one of the very few truisms in the special events endeavor, one it shares with the entire universe:

> Nature may loath a vacuum, but it LOVES lethargy.

Including the human variety, nature tends to take it easy. Solar systems take eons to mature – about as plodding as actions by many boards. Most people, along with board members, generally don't enjoy making decisions, and so they're slow at it—or, as in the Ms. D's case, they grind to a dead stop. Don't expect a two-minute discussion followed by a unanimous decision favoring your new plan. It's just not very likely to happen.

One of several talents found in the consummate special events practitioner is the fine art of The Compromise. This capability is indispensable in a volunteer-driven pursuit. Remember, everyone from boards of directors to the guys and gals in the trenches are donating perhaps their three most precious possessions: TIME—TOIL—TALENT. And they are doing so without pay. Be prepared to negotiate your reformation plan. Rarely does one get adopted in its original form.

WORKING OUT "TURFISM" SPASMS

"That's in *my* area. Mess with it and you die."

Jurisdictional uprisings can send wild-eyed, torch-bearing, hyper-hyper villagers scurrying up the hill to your castle in a matter of minutes. Such actions can often be prevented or squelched by the simple expediency of fairly detailed written Committee Descriptions.[4] If Ms. Desperate doesn't have a sufficiently encompassing CD for each of her groups, she should remedy that situation at once. And you should, too—before disputes arise. And they will.

If D. and you have a set of CD's, examine them regularly to be sure they're up-to-date and satisfactorily comprehensive. When a new responsibility raises its hand for attention, give it that attention. Write it down and assign it immediately.

Really important: You and Ms. Desperate should be sure that every one of your Chairholders has copies of *all current* CD's. Tell each that you fully expect him/her to be thoroughly knowledgeable about all CD contents and to raise any questions, especially jurisdictional ones, *now*. Whenever there is any addition, deletion or change in definitions, get the revised CD's into the hands of all committee heads immediately.

If they do their jobs as they should, those Chairholders will see to it that their volunteers are knowledgeable about all Committee Descriptions, especially new versions.

CD's aren't answers to every need or problem. But they certainly do help.

MEET MS. RUTHLESS AND MR. MONSTER

Talk about attitude! You haven't *seen* attitude until you meet these two people. With them it has to be genetic. Ms. Ruthless and Mr. Monster are so bad even the zodiac doesn't have a sign for them. On their best-behavior days, their objective is to make everyone they encounter entirely miserable, depressed, frustrated and just plain wretched. They're always successful.

Before they exhibited this severe flaw, each managed to land a volunteer position in Ms. Desperate's event. Lucky her. Now what can she do about them? Although more and more frequently employed these days, murder is still bad PR. And since they're volunteers, she can't fire 'em.

Oh, yes she can—and should! Fire them, I mean. *Nobody's fire-proof*, not even unpaid volunteers.

If she's exercised every effort to find and have them apply their good points without any success, she should fire 'em. Best approach is to have the chairholder of a *board* committee or leading administrator(s), together with the primary complainant(s), meet with these two offenders and explain as quietly and succinctly as possible that they are being asked to leave the organization and why. They can be offered the resignation option, but Desperate & Co. should be firm in their decision to have that pair removed from the organization one way or another. Permanently.

"But Ruthless is the chamber president's daughter and Monster is the mayor's nephew. Now, what can I do?," she wept.

YOU MAY HAVE TO USE THE SNAKE

If Desperate's convinced that outright firing isn't an option, she should give them a fancy new title and then institute "snaking."

Having absolutely nothing to do with reptile-hunting, snaking is an ancient and dishonorable weapon used by those who can. It's the practice of giving the very worst possible jobs in a stack of assignments to others than yourself or those who kiss up to you.

In the event-volunteer world "indispensable" snakable jobs usually include anything that has to do with the event but is terminally boring, like counting something—ticket stubs; people (with one of those little thumb-tiring hand clicker-counters); paper clips, pencils and other bzillion-tiny-unit supplies; tissue sheets for portable potties; number of vehicles in the parking lot; etc. Other snakables are inspecting site conditions, *after* each day's cleanup, and writing a report (could take from midnight to dawn) to some empty-titled exec; examining tent conditions four times daily and writing a report to some empty-titled exec; frequent personal inspections of each operating entity and writing a report to . . . well, you get the idea.

Okay, if firing isn't feasible and snaking doesn't work, Desperate has a third possibility: elevate them to an empty-titled job to whom many others write critical, entirely meaningless reports, which need to be summarized and handed to her on a critical time basis.

Americans are title-happy. Believe it. An Executive Assistant Something Or Other or a Chairholder of Such-and-Such are giant ego inflatables. If they run true to form, Ruthless and Monster will wallow in their perceived elevations, complete with shining new titles. They might even shut up . . . or they might not.

When all else has failed, she should fold in the old fashioned silent treatment. Harsh? Perhaps. But why should these extra difficult people be tolerated to the detriment of an entire organization and the enjoyment of a great many constituents? They deserve ostracism.

Hizzoner and the chamber prez may exert lay-off pressure. Try explaining the importance of their new positions, that they are "indispensable responsibilities that can be handled only by those with the highest qualifications." If that doesn't work . . . well, you've done your best.

"VIRULENT OWNERSHIP"

One of the most viciously voracious viruses attacking special event bodies manifests itself by endowing its victims with superhuman grips on "their" event assignments. It enables them to resist any change, even improvements (they normally won't admit improvements are possible), or—God forbid!—replacement of those elements.

"Virulent Ownership" frequently happens when the same people are allowed to function in the same function in your function year after year. They contribute countless hours—and maybe even bucks—to what then becomes "theirs." It's quite natural for them to assume full proprietorship, but it's rarely good for the overall event.

On the surface it would seem that such a combination of dedication and loyalty should be commended, to be rewarded, certainly emulated. Fine, so long as it doesn't become a neurosis, as so often happens.

Ms. Desperate should have stopped VO before it started by rotating all appropriate assignments with reasonable frequency. In an annual event, people should be moved around about every two years — three max; some do it annually. Reassignments should be time-staggered to avoid a year without experience in any particular area. Personnel rotation also assures new blood and new thinking for all your event elements.

Now that VO has smashed into D's event, she'll either have to bite the symbolic bullet—or use it figuratively to shoot a hole in that tenacious hold.

Nobody ever said people management is easy; sometimes you simply *must* make an unpleasant removal (see Ruthless/Monster section above) for the overall betterment of your event.

BATTLING BATTLE-BOUND BOARDS

Let us all give thanks also for the thousands of good, qualified people who give up so much of their time and contribute so much talent to our event boards of directors. Quite simply, ladies and gentlemen, we couldn't do it without you.

By far, the great majority of these folks have the best interests of the events they serve at heart. I have met board members who have put in efforts, dedication and loyalty easily worthy of big-time CEO-size salaries.

As is true in industry, however, there are board members, such as those strangling Ms. Desperate's event, who are greater hazards than helpers. This usually is the result of self-interests trampling best event-interests.

Face it. There really is very little anyone can do about a board of directors choked into inaction by internal bickering, strife, politics and turf protectionism. Except the board itself.

Ever since Watergate gave us modern investigative reporting, media have reveled in bringing the focus of ugly public attention on their "gotcha" findings. Sometimes, those actions correct the faulty situations. Am I suggesting that Ms. Desperate seek media aid in breaking this gridlock? Only if she feels comfortable—and safe—in doing so.

WHY MICRO IS SO MACRO

Indecision and inaction are only two of three major afflictions binding so many boards of directors. Possibly, the third is even more debilitating; it's one of our most crippling and chronic epidemics: *micromanagement.*

Consider these mini-excerpts from case histories of this horror I have encountered, even before hearing Ms. D's testimony:

— One board spent almost four months mulling over (and finally mauling) an excellent poster/t-shirt design contributed by a fully qualified, truly talented graphic artist. Results: (1) something between a design mutation and an abomination that (2) caused artists to shun that event the following two or three years, which (3) led to shameful graphics year after year.

— Another was bound and gagged far too long over whether official stationery should be printed on lightly tinted or stark white stock. Cost difference was not the pivot, aesthetic factors (read that "personal desires") were.

— A third was enmeshed so much in conflict over the wording of a volunteer thank-you letter that it formed a task force of its own members to formulate the message. It took more than six weeks for that group to submit its best suggestion, which was rejected by the board, which sent it back to the task force, which worked on it some more and re-submitted it to the board, which finally gave approval to a letter, which went out nearly three months after the event served by those volunteers.

Every event board should have this message done in needlepoint, framed, hung in their meeting room, and repeated right after the Pledge of Allegiance at every meeting:

> **I am not here to serve and please ME.**
>
> **I am here to please those I SERVE.**

One more equally important suggestion about event boards: more entertainment, creative people should be appointed to them. Too many boards encompass too many "administrators," those champions of industry deemed boardable because they apparently know how to run things. And that's good . . . up to a point. But chancing allegations of stereotyping, I contend that most of those captains (or even generals) of industry haven't a clue as to what entertains people—no sense of the dramatic, no flair for the spectacle, no comprehension of program balance, no feel for satisfying and pleasing crowds of people.

Keeping within budgets is not the first, not the primary purpose—nor the *raison d'étre*—of special events. Rather, it's to have a quality event *within* a budget. To make every dollar do the work of two . . . or three . . . or more.

THE POLITICAL GODFATHER

I have found very few cases of effective administration of an event by chambers of commerce, city councils, or other organizations whose first responsibility is other than running that event. It's best, by far, to start an event's life on its own; if it's already in existence, the earlier the break, the easier the break.

Ms. Desperate's case, however, is past the young-life stage. And, unfortunately, like the Bickering Board, the heavily entrenched Political Godfather organizational hold will be very hard to rub out (figuratively, of course). My only suggestion to her is to get all facts together that she can think of to demonstrate how much more effectively and efficiently her event would function if it were its own boss—an independent corporation, organized in compliance with the rules of one of the Internal Revenue Service's 501 categories. Ms. D. should emphasize that her independent group will continue to cooperate with the former parent—and do so.

If Ms. Desperate can find one or more leading business persons who are sympathetic to her cause, their influence with "the owner" can be very valuable. Also, if there are independent events in her area, you might ask them to share the advantages of such freedom with her and her parent organization.

(Of course, it just may be that your particular happening works well having its organization under such parental authority. If so, great, but keep your eye on things.)

SO WHAT'S NEW? NOTHING!

Stagnation almost always results from the presence of all or many of the above-listed afflictions. It is a disease every bit as lethal as Virulent Ownership to which stagnation is especially closely related.

If Ms. Desperate can get her group to try these solutions, they will almost certainly begin to function more successfully (probably pretty slowly at first) and they will find creativity beginning to show up again. Morale will also brighten and the infusion of new ideas will bring new public program offerings. Attendance is virtually certain to pick up, all other things being equal. And sponsorship levels can be expected to improve, both in terms of new supporter additions and dollar increases from those who've remained faithful to her ailing event.

RECRUITING EXECUTIVE VOLUNTEERS

Enough for now about Ms. Desperate's existing issues. Let's look at some measures she—and you—can take to derail other fairly common problems even before they arise.

Any group of people assigned a common task must be managed to some degree or other. My usual recommendation to clients is to have volunteers managed by executive volunteers, who, in turn, are managed by the board of directors through the paid staff. Reasons? There are usually too few salaried staff members to supervise effectively even a moderately sized volunteer body while trying to carry out the myriad duties required in the overall picture. Further, it is usually more palatable for volunteers to have unpaid individuals supervising them.

Executive volunteers, then, take on exceptionally important roles. As such, it's imperative that the right people fill the right managerial positions. Here are a series of guidelines designed to help recruit the best people-managers:

— **Look for candidates who are *very* busy.** Cliché though it may be, it's still valid. Interestingly, these remarkably busy people most often serve as exceptionally effective executive volunteers. Why? To start with, they're invariably masters of time use and work efficiency, the basics of efficient operations.

— **Strongly consider those who are not known for volunteering**. They may be supremely qualified but have been overlooked or approached wrongly, disappointed in previous volunteering roles, or they have just never found an opportunity that interested them. Your approach and event may be just what they've been waiting for, so go get 'em.

— When appropriate, point out that **executive volunteer positions with your event are going to be very desirable** and brightly colored feathers in professional caps. Emphasize that your event will have such dimensions that serving it will be a major highlight on anyone's résumé or brochure of professional experiences. It could also help them attract customers, consumers, clients, patients, etc. Crass but true . . . an effective recruiting lever.

— Point out an indisputable fact: that **volunteering for your event is a significant means of contributing to the betterment of the community**. Tell them that freely-given time, efforts and talent are as worthwhile and commendable—are just as valuable and rewarding—as providing such services for any other altruistic, humanitarian endeavor.

— Although you should seek people who know how to work *very hard,* be sure to **recruit those *who also know how to have fun while they're working.*** I'll remind you again: special events staffed by people who *really* enjoy their work inevitably sparkle with sparks of success.

— In initial contacts, attempt to **determine right off if there are any known impediment**s *that cannot be removed,* which would interfere with their full and total implementation of event responsibilities. Commitment extends from earliest need through post-event clean-up and wrap-up. Obstacles to look out for are long-planned lengthy vacations (more than a couple of consecutive weeks); births; marriages and honeymoons; school requirements; heavier-than-usual business or professional demands (work loads, special projects, lengthy or frequent travel); etc. If so, (a) see if obstacles can be removed; (b) determine whether steps can be taken to get the volunteer job done fully, effectively and pleasantly along with or in spite of those obstacles, (c) have in mind a lesser role an especially qualified candidate-volunteer might play if obstacles to a higher responsibility can't be removed, or (d) if that person absolutely cannot fit into a volunteer position, ask if he/she might recommend someone who can.

MINING FOR VOLUNTEERS

Where do you find volunteers? Wherever you let it be known that you need them. It's like being unemployed; the more people who know you're job-prospecting, the more likely you are to hit pay dirt. Here are some source categories that have worked for events:

— Publicity, advertising and PSAs (see Chapter 4)

— Speakers Bureau (another Chapter 4 tool)

— Church and school contacts

— Recruiting announcements at meetings of civic, fraternal, professional, support group, etc. organizations

— Suppliers—those who sell you their goods and services; they can often be excellent sources of personpower.

— Mentions at home-owners association meetings

— Cards on supermarket and other store community-service message boards

— Months before they're needed, hold a Volunteer Recruitment Reception, inviting every breathing human available, through heavy publicity and PSA's (see Chapter 4).

— With the crossover into the 21st Century, more and more baby boomers will come of age—*retirement* age. Go after them! There's already a new kind of senior citizen out there. You young whippersnappers may be surprised to learn that many of the current and coming gray generations do not retreat to the rocker, shawl around shoulders, tiny glasses perched on nose-tip, and worn brown house slippers warming feet chilled by bad circulation. Most are spunky, entirely able-bodied, maximum functioning people. They'll have more time than was available in their younger years, and most will be financially stable, if not exactly wealthy. All the right stuff for volunteerism. They're walking silver (haired) mines!

VOLUNTEER PERKS

With the plethora of volunteer-driven organizations in existence now, which will certainly grow in number in the new Century, you must be prepared to outdo your competition in attractiveness, if you want to get sufficient numbers of the *best* executive as well as line volunteers. You can do it largely with perks—until your competition catches on and matches your favors, then you may have to resort to even more creative measures. But for now, here are some suggestions for volunteer perks:

— Canvass food vendors in an effort to find one or more who might be willing to pack tasty, filling—but really inexpensive—box or other types of lunches, available only on the presentation of official volunteer credentials.

— Check with beverage vendors; some might make drinks available either free or at reduced prices for volunteers only.

— Ask merchandise vendors if they would be willing to grant a discount to those who qualify as full-time volunteers.

— Some community-minded stores, shops, restaurants or services might be talked into offering special price treatments to holders of volunteer certification. Especially if they're exhibitors in or sponsors of your event.

— If you're rich enough, you might give food and beverage script (see No. 4, Chapter 7) at low or no cost to volunteers

— Is there an opportunity to upgrade your uniforms, making them the most attractive in town? You might be surprised at how important this perk is to many volunteers.

— Add a cap, hat or umbrella, generously denoting "Volunteer."

— Arrange for the most convenient parking available to be reserved for credential-bearing volunteers.

— Contact your metropolitan transportation authority and ask if it will make bus rides to and from the event free or at reduced cost to volunteers.

— If you have large areas of seating, set aside a generous number for first-come-first-served volunteers—and their families, if possible.

— Be sure to have more than enough security around when volunteers finish late shifts. After dark, offer security escorts to parked automobiles, bus stops and pedestrian pick-up points.

— Heavily promote carpooling. Not only is it efficient transportation, but volunteers enjoy each other's company. A real morale boost . . . lots of fun.

— If you're large enough that you have event-end auctions to get rid of God-knows-what, arrange a closed session ahead of the public offering—just for your volunteers, of course.

— Annually, give the best Volunteer Appreciation Party in the history of special events. And be sure to include a wildly generous series of drawings for really cool prizes.

MANAGING VOLUNTEERS

Carefully practiced management is particularly essential when working effectively with non-paid "employees." These marvelous people very often do work worth mountainous salaries, their reward often being only the inner glow they enjoy by making a selfless contribution of self.

It may not seem so, but this is a compliment to volunteers: management must allow about twice the time for volunteers to accomplish the same task as if it were performed by paid employees. In addition to regular jobs, most of these folks have commitments to family, church, school, community, and possibly other altruistic pursuits, all of which demand that most precious of all possessions, *time.* They can give only so much to your endeavor, and "outside" interruptions must not be just tolerated, but expected and willingly accommodated. Thus, the twice-as-much-time formula must always be operable.

If there is one event management flaw that is worse than giving volunteers *too much* to do, it's giving them *too little* to do. People who've made known their wishes to be of service will not stay around long if those wishes aren't fulfilled. Our basic human need to be needed is almost an instinct, but, interestingly, it's especially powerful in most volunteers. They have felt it so strongly that they have openly and actively expressed it. They have *volunteered.*

SHIFTS, TO THE RIGHT DECISION

Some established events steadfastly resist the idea of asking volunteers to serve in shifts. One of the most frequently given reasons is that more volunteers are needed and "it's hard enough as it is to get enough people to work with us."

Interestingly, I have noted that many having shift assignments found the opposite to be true. They were able to recruit more people who were willing to devote, say, four hours at a time, rather than eight or more at a stretch. And still more interestingly, many veteran volunteers signed up for more on-job hours than they were giving because they could "break up" their service into smaller time chunks. Those who preferred longer work spans simply signed up for two or three consecutive shifts. Short-hour stints give a flexibility that often meshes well with other personal demands, which underlies their general popularity.

True of all matters, shifts don't work for every event, but don't pooh-pooh the idea before you've investigated it thoroughly. You could be surprised.

And like most other practices, this suggestion isn't perfect; among the drawbacks:

— **More parking may be required** since incoming volunteers must somewhat overlap take-over time when relieving those leaving. This may be greatly alleviated by the simple expedience of *strongly encouraging volunteer carpooling* which should be a part of your volunteer program anyway. Easy shuttling is another answer.

— **There are more people to train**. However, in carefully planned and timed training sessions, twenty people can be as easily trained as ten, fifty, a hundred or more.

But even with these drawbacks, volunteer shift grids virtually always produce more happiness than unhappiness.

LET'S TALK TRAINING

Properly preparing volunteers for their jobs is one of the most important considerations in the events industry. Alas, too frequently volunteers are told in a few sentences what to do—then turned loose to do it. Or they are domino-trained; they work a few minutes at the side of someone supposedly qualified in a job, who had worked a few minutes at the side of someone supposedly qualified in a job, who had worked . . . and on down the line.

Healthy training programs take time, but they pay off. Here are a few ingredients in good training strategies:

— Offer more than one training time-option. Giving alternative meeting opportunities almost always increases participation.

— Provide a suitable training site, atmosphere and arrangements.

√ Select most likely times to attract participants

√ Schedule training to take place just before it's needed in the event

√ Emphasize the need to wear appropriate, comfortable clothes

√ Provide a map or clearly-given written directions to the location

√ Give contacts and telephone numbers along with the map/directions

√ A must: plenty of parking, well-lighted at night, and otherwise secure

√ Sufficient room to do whatever is needed to train attendees

√ Ideally, training should take place where volunteers will work

√ Offer a baby-sitting option—in a nearby but separate area from the actual training site

√   Provide lapel name tags

√   Assign each new volunteer to a veteran for "buddy" purposes

√   Hand out a training outline, which can be filled in by trainees

√   That outline or a narrative you provide should be valuable on the job

√   Try to assure comfortable room temperature

√   Make light refreshments available

√   Strongly encourage questions; even plant some to break the ice

√   Keep each training session to a maximum of sixty to ninety minutes

√   Plan more than one session (but not more than two or three) if one hour to an hour and a half is insufficient.

— Be sure you have the right people assigned to the right jobs from the outset. Interviews should follow completion of application forms prepared by each candidate volunteers. If the applicant isn't sure what role is suitable, give him/her a list of thumbnail descriptions of committees having openings. Ask each applicant to select a first, second and third choice. (Even after the most careful placement procedures, some volunteers will end up in the wrong slots. Waste no time in correcting those misfittings.)

— Provide well qualified instructors to conduct training in their specialized areas. Volunteers who've proved their capabilities often make good teachers. Also, consider enlisting the help from local professionals with specific expertise, asking them to meet with their group counterparts two or three times at the outset of event planning.

— Prepare clearly stated, concise Position Descriptions for *every* assignment. These should be segments that add up to your overall Committee Descriptions. You might be surprised at the number of questions that need answering when you start preparing these write-ups—and other answers that must be found when PD's are put into action. By the way, plan a second writing of a new PD, based on those matters that come up when it's had on-the-job use. It's almost inevitable.

— Hand out applicable PD's to your volunteers either at sign-up times or when assignments are handed out, then review them in group training sessions for that particularly job classification or in person if sessions aren't appropriate.

AN EXECUTIVE COUNCIL? CONSIDER IT

For organizations of five or six or more committees, I recommend establishment of an Executive Council. Ordinarily, every Chairholder is a member of an EC, chaired by the event's board president or highest paid executive. On some occasions, an organization could be presided over by an executive volunteer.

Purpose of this organization is to provide maximum coordination of all event activities. It also is charged with:

— Negotiating solutions to disputes, committee jurisdictional questions, crises, problems and any other significant matters faced by the event as a whole or by individual committees

— Serving as the primary feeder source for the event stable of speakers (see Chapter 4)

— Providing the governing person or body with input on any subject that person or body requests, including, but not limited to:

√   Assigning, reassigning or deleting committee and individual responsibilities and duties

√   Proposing steps to strengthen working relationships within and among the various committees

√   Taking whatever measures are necessary to ensure continuing improvement of event from year to year

√   Designing and supervising a general volunteers meeting immediately after each event, to discuss strengths and weaknesses while details are still fresh in volunteer minds

√   Preparing and hosting a post-event volunteer appreciation and honors party

NOTES ON FOLLOWING COMMITTEE DESCRIPTIONS

Although the forthcoming descriptions are based on considerable previous experience and years of study, modifications will be required to fit the needs of each individual event. Descriptions given below are designed to serve as workable bases for satisfying fundamental needs of a typical mid-size happening. They also demonstrate with maximum emphasis the interrelationships of the various organizational units.

In addition to their individualized responsibilities, all committees should:

— have all positions filled by a board or executive-given deadline, each being selected and trained in conjunction with the Human Relations Committee

— prepare a concise but reasonably complete Post-Event Review (PER) report, designed to enable committees to function more effectively in the next go-round or to document the part each played in a one-time event

— participate in post-event clean-up, designed to return event site(s), borrowed equipment, material, etc. to pre-use condition

COMMITTEE DESCRIPTIONS

Along with a job summary of a paid Executive Director, here are Committee Descriptions that can also serve as Position Descriptions for those committee Chairholders. In turn, descriptions should be broken down and somewhat more fleshed out to become individual Position Descriptions for each volunteer committee member.

"Quality Protection Chairholder and Committee," as its own unit, may be quite new to many events, its duties being shared presently and in the past by other functions. However, as more and more need for improved overall event quality is recognized, I predict that it will become a standard operating unit by early in the next century. That is why I have given it a high-up position in this descriptions list.

Committees thereafter are presented more or less in a random order based on use frequency, although they share (or should) absolutely equal billings in most instances—Marketing, Sponsorship, Site Preparations, Maintenance, Finance, Vendors, Human Resources, Supplies, Transportation, Communications, Security and Safety, and certainly Entertainment.

Completing the list are committees that are up-and-coming in terms of importance, likely becoming standard event inclusions in the next few years. They are Group Attendance, Hospitality, Event Extension, Sports (obviously a specialty), and Awards and Prizes.

> FORMAT NOTE: It may seem that I have suspended the maximum-white-space characteristic of Power Writing (see Chapter 4) in the following descriptions. I have. (You will recall that I emphatically stated that Power Writing isn't suited to every use; here's one.) My primary reason is that you aren't expected to absorb the hundreds of details in these segments; you need be only familiar enough with "where they are" to find information you will need when preparing your RFP response. These descriptions are research and reference instruments, not sell or communications paragraphs, per se. And the printer is also yelling about space limitations. Enough excuses?

EXECUTIVE DIRECTOR

PREFERRED QUALITIES: event managerial experience highly desirable; should be especially gifted with a sense of interpersonal communications for reaching and persuading; extraordinary people skills essential; wide range of local personal and professional contacts of value to event is a plus; should be self-starter with strong follow-through habits; must be able to handle crisis developments; close ties with community leaders is definite plus; operational versatility and flexibility are high-priority requirements, as is willingness to put in long hours doing hard work.

STAFF DESCRIPTION: Serves as a full-time paid staff member; works closely with board and all executive volunteers; oversees all financial and budgetary matters with Finance Chairholder; assures maximum functioning of returning units within budgetary allocations and policy directions decreed by the board; assists board and executive volunteers in resolving any inter-committee disputes; generally, handles the day-to-day event operations; makes policy, organizational and procedural recommendations to board; and, generally carries out assignments given by board. Reports directly to board of directors.

EXECUTIVE VOLUNTEER

For smaller events or those not ready to hire an Executive Director, this is a suggested *interim* position until the permanent paid position can become a reality. Qualifications and duties are the same as for the Executive Director.

QUALITY PROTECTION CHAIRHOLDER AND COMMITTEE

DESIRED EXPERIENCE: Supervisory experience in corporate quality control operations or contract negotiations committee; professional middle- to upper-level management experience important; should possess significant people skills; demonstrates ability to be "friendly but firm" in handling situations not meeting prescribed event standards.

POSITION DESCRIPTION: Serves as de facto Assistant Executive Chairholder (may have volunteer assistants, as desired); helps establish very high but reasonable quality standards in terms of all "presentation" aspects of event—its general "look," nature and condition of venues, tents and all other shelters, and grounds, demeanor of volunteers; oversees full compliance with all governmental regulations and ordinances (health, safety, food, etc.); responsible for obtaining all necessary licenses, permits, inspection documents, etc., and seeing that all are strictly adhered to; obtains sufficient insurance; VERY IMPORTANT—assures that no event action or lack of action will result in injury to the environment or its inhabitants in any manner whatsoever; assures that all areas meet or exceed minimum state and federal requirements for wheelchair and handicap accessibility; must assure that women and minorities are given full access to all positions; required to work pleasantly but firmly with all committees, especially closely with entertainment, vendors, construction, transportation, security and safety, and maintenance, which will mean often attending those and other committee meetings; works with executive council, Executive Chairholder and Executive Director to resolve significant disputes, crises, problems, obstacles, etc. Reports directly to the Executive Director or event Executive Chairholder.

MARKETING CHAIRHOLDER AND COMMITTEE[5]

DESIRED EXPERIENCE: Essential to have professional marketing experience, with special strengths in publicity/media relations; designing and implementing promotions; written, verbal and exceptional people skills are required; advertising, marketing research and graphics background definite pluses; national-scope experience may eventually be put to strong use; must be capable of developing and implementing especially creative concepts and their implementation in all event work; should be knowledgeable in use of new, high-tech means of widespread communications (faxes, Internet, etc.)

COMMITTEE DESCRIPTION: Handles all media activities for entire event, including but not limited to news conferences, preparation of print and air media material (scripts, fact sheets, releases, photos, captions, etc.) video preparations for media *and all other event uses;* works closely with Hospitality Chairholder and committee on arrangements for media services and media accessibility; garners general positive relations with all media personnel, including those on management levels in television and radio stations, as well as newspapers and magazines; devises and implements effective, wide-ranging event speakers bureau (functioning from late the year before until just before event Day One each year, with the Executive Director or event executive council serving as the primary feeder group of speakers); establishes and maintains strong, effective working relationship with local and state departments of tourism and similar organizations, to create joint promotional material and programs designed to increase attendance and widespread recognition of event; arranges for local and state governments to pass proclamations recognizing event; designs and places any and all advertisements, commercials, and especially, public service announcements (printed and aired); determines and arranges for all technical needs of media covering event; sets up media-involvement procedures in the event of crises; effectively uses fairly recently developed means of mass communication (faxes, Internet, etc.) to spread event promotional publicity; assists through media with recruiting (for volunteers, entertainers, sports participants, etc.); designs and distributes pre-event newsletter to always-current local, regional, statewide and (when applicable) national mailing lists; responsible for creation and legal protection (copyrights [©], trademarks [™], registered [®], of all graphic arts, including logos, symbols, stationery, T-shirts, posters, lapel buttons, etc.; responsible for all photography, poster distribution, videotaping and printing, including the official event souvenir program and/or newspaper supplements; arranges for selling advertising for and production of the official event program, as well as its sales and distribution. Reports directly to the Executive Director or event Executive Chairholder.

SPONSORSHIP CHAIRHOLDER AND COMMITTEE

DESIRED EXPERIENCE: Must be the consummate salesperson with vision, able to sell ideas and concepts to potential sponsors; choice verbal and people skills an indispensable requirement; especially thorough knowledge of local commercial community a definite plus, as are solid connections with business leaders.

COMMITTEE DESCRIPTION: Obtains major national and local, all-price levels of sponsorship funding; plans and implements an ambitious program to produce sponsorship contributions—monetary and in-kind— from merchants and all other commercial, for-profit organizations in the surrounding area and, when applicable, throughout the nation; works closely with Hospitality Chairholder and committee in providing all hosting needs and services for representatives from sponsoring organizations, including but not limited to special audience seating in designated, sponsor-assigned sections for all performances; assumes full responsibility for improving and enlarging programs that solicit various levels of corporate and individual donations other than sponsorships, per se; credentialing (with Security and Safety Chairholder and committee), special parking and transportation arrangements (with Transportation Chairholder and committee); working with Site Preparations Chairholder and committee, causes the development and displaying of sponsor banners and any other related signage; guarantees safety of attending sponsees and their guests, in cooperation with the Security and Safety Chairholder and committee; assures that appropriate, agreed-to sponsor credit is given in all event-generated communications and signage opportunities; works in tandem with Awards and Prizes Chairholder and committee in their pursuit of contributed or lowered-cost items from those who should be listed and treated as sponsors. Reports directly to Executive Director or Executive Chairholder.

SITE PREPARATIONS CHAIRHOLDER AND COMMITTEE

DESIRED EXPERIENCE: Professional artistic designer, decorator (interior and/or exterior) or architect; demonstrates ability to be especially creative in arranging for or designing and placing of architectural elements and decorative materials and plants; ideally, experienced in crowd-flow patterns, balancing structural spatial relationships, utilizing colors for maximum appeal and positive influence, and providing quality results with budget-limited production.

COMMITTEE DESCRIPTION: Creates, produces, places and removes all on-site architectural and decorative elements; works out arrangements with local merchants, communities and, if appropriate, off-site sports and other venues to display committee-produced banners, signs and decorations; cooperates closely with Marketing Chairholder and committee in all matters regarding display or any uses of event graphics; solicits resources to donate or significantly reduce costs of construction and decorations materials (with Sponsorship Chairholder and committee); serves event landscaping volunteers as their liaison with event management and arranges with them for all landscaping; devises and implements design plan to guarantee important cohesive "look" of event; provides equipment and labor to build structures and place all decorations effectively and safely (with Safety and Security Chairholder and committee) and to permit easy replacement in the event of theft or damage; responsible for removal of all items placed by Site Preparations Chairholder and committee following event; designs, constructs and maintains all structures, including but not limited to tents, kiosk-type buildings, performance stages, platforms, signage and decoration frames, flooring, barriers and barricades, bridges, walkways and paths, gateways, temporary vehicle road surfacing, lighting and sound structural supports, handicap accessible requirements, counters and flat working surfaces (does not include items for food, beverage or merchandise vendors), folding and fixed chairs, tables, supports or frames for backdrops or stage paneling (under the direction of Entertainment Chairholder and committee); arranges for equipment to meet all electrical needs—generators and/ or cable drops—doing so with objective being to obtain such equipment at low or no cost; responsible for all event warehousing needs; expected to solicit construction materials at low or no cost; responsible for acquiring, also at no or low cost, all equipment, supplies and tools required for all Site preparations Committee work. Reports directly to Executive Director or Executive Chairholder.

MAINTENANCE CHAIRHOLDER AND COMMITTEE

PREFERRED BACKGROUND: Mid-level or high managerial position with building and grounds maintenance operation, janitorial service or structural rehabilitation effort; involvement in recycling and other environmental protection processes especially helpful.

COMMITTEE DESCRIPTION: Organizes and supervises all maintenance facilities; fully responsible for assuring at all times the cleanliness and clutter-free condition of event sites (including cooperation with any off-site sports or other venues), before, during and after event; assures that no odors exist, especially near food areas; supervises post-event clean-up with the help of all committees; assures that each venue is returned to pre-event use; studies and provides recycling efforts to dispose of as much refuse as possible; arranges for, places and overseas care of satellite toilets; arranges for *frequent* trash removal; works especially closely with Site Preparations, Quality Assurance and Security and Safety Chairholders and committees. Reports directly to the Executive Director or Executive Chairholder.

FINANCE CHAIRHOLDER AND COMMITTEE

DESIRED EXPERIENCE: Mid- to upper-level management in the capacity of a Certified Public Accountant[6], professional auditor or accountant, corporate treasurer or similar; should be a financial/budgetary expert, accustomed to operating effectively on a very limited budget.

COMMITTEE DESCRIPTION: Serves as developer and overseer of event budget; works with Executive Director, Executive Chairholder, and each committee Chairholder to develop a workable budget for all operating units, in conformity with financial allocations provided for each committee by board action; administers all accounting practices and procedures; responsible for all tax related matters; provides a budgetary report periodically, as prescribed by board action; responsible for all banking arrangements; provides for protection of any cash on hand; sets up cash-flow and script control; prepares and submits financial statements as required by the board. Reports directly to the Executive Director or Executive Chairholder.

VENDOR CHAIRHOLDER AND COMMITTEE

PREFERRED BACKGROUND: Organizes and supervises all central and any satellite food and beverage areas; managerial committee for retail sales, merchandise display and promotion, or food service. (Because of the need for expertise in each of these fields, it may be the option of the Vendors Chairholder, who will manage all event-celebrants sales activities, to recruit two Assistant Chairholders, one for consumables, the other for merchandise.)

COMMITTEE DESCRIPTION: Designs, arranges and manages central and all satellite food and beverage facilities, assuring that vendors arrange for appropriate equipment and furnishings; organizes and manages all official event merchandise centers and satellites; sees that all merchandise vendors are provided with appropriate equipment and furnishings; provides sale or rental of foldable lawn chairs, pallets, umbrellas, and other items as needed for diner comfort; handles all aspects of sales of event lapel buttons and all other official event merchandise on-site and throughout community before and during event; works directly with Finance Chairholder and committee to assure proper accounting for sales and protection of cash (along with Safety and Security Chairholder and committee); studies and applies best formula for sale and collection procedures for food and beverage script[7]; provides proper facilities and their placement to sell and service vendor operations; works with Maintenance Chairholder and committee, to assure that all food areas are spotless and odor-free *at all times*; working with Quality Protection Chairholder and committee; assures that all permits are obtained and areas are always in compliance with laws, ordinances and permit specifications; cooperates with Transportation Chairholder and committee to develop plans for handling vendor service vehicles and merchandise/food storage immediately before and during event. Reports directly to Executive Director or Executive Chairholder.

HUMAN RESOURCES CHAIRHOLDER AND COMMITTEE

DESIRED EXPERIENCE: Mid- to upper-level management of human resources department or organization; ideally, has worked extensively and successfully with volunteers; must possess the best of all attributes required for successfully working with people, especially volunteers; acceptable level of knowledge of labor laws and organized labor requirements; mediation skills should be well honed.

COMMITTEE DESCRIPTION: Organizes and manages all volunteer-related duties and facilities; assists each Chairholder with recruiting, screening, placing, training and generally managing volunteers, including dismissal of poorly performing personnel; recruits and maintains a pool of general service volunteers who can be called on to serve on committees, permanently, temporarily or sequentially to perform interim "spot jobs;" maintains fully adequate volunteer personnel files; should be called on to participate in speakers bureau at opportunities for recruitment; deals with all matters related to organized labor; with Executive Director or Executive Chairholder, responsible for the design and distribution of volunteer identification apparel—t-shirts, sashes etc.; provides for any volunteer credentialing in concert with Safety and Security Chairholder and committee; plans and implements the post-event Volunteer Appreciation and Recognition Party. Reports directly to Executive Director or Executive Chairholder.

SUPPLIES CHAIRHOLDER AND COMMITTEE

DESIRED EXPERIENCE: Purchasing agent or official, office supplier, retail or wholesale sales or purchasing executive.

COMMITTEE DESCRIPTION: Organizes and manages all supplies-related storage and distribution areas; serves as general purchasing agent for entire event for basic, tangible operational needs—office supplies, Duct®Tape, rope, etc.; sets up well-controlled procedure for ordering, distributing and retrieving unused items; purchases awards and prizes in conjunction with Awards and Prizes Chairholder and committee; expected to fulfill needs at low or no cost; sets up effective procedure for accountability of all purchased or donated items; works out warehousing needs with Site Preparations Chairholder and committee; works on expenditures planning and accounting with Finance Chairholder and committee. NOTE: does not purchase or rent: any items used by construction personnel nor such specialized or intangibles as advertising space, TV time, special services, nor performance-related specialized items, including lighting and sound equipment, etc., nor any other items exempted by Executive Director or Executive Chairholder. Reports directly to the Executive Director or Executive Chairholder.

TRANSPORTATION CHAIRHOLDER AND COMMITTEE

DESIRED EXPERIENCE: Mid- to upper-level management in a rapid transit, public transportation operation, or law enforcement agency or private enterprise dealing with traffic, parking, motor pools, etc.

COMMITTEE DESCRIPTION: Organizes and manages all transportation-related operational and storage areas; handles all aspects of vehicle movement and parking; working with Vendor Chairholder and committee, designs and implements carefully created plan to handle vendor supply vehicles before, during and after event; works with Site Preparations Chairholder and committee to satisfy needs for preparing grass lots and/or other spaces for parking; sets up arrangements for parking in established lots near event site(s); works with Security and Safety Chairholder and committee on protection of vehicles and safe movement of pedestrians; in tandem with Executive Director or Executive Chairholder and Sponsorship Chairholder and committee, attempts to arrange for and be in full control of rented, leased, loaned or donated automobiles, trucks, golf carts, bicycles, busses, trailers, traffic-control devices, traffic signals/

signs, fuel, etc.; sets up and operates efficiently any shuttle services; arranges preferential parking accommodations for all event volunteers, media, VIPs and sponsors; arranges for movement of volunteers between event-occupied sites; should attempt implementation of all responsibilities at low or no cost. Reports directly to Executive Director or Executive Chairholder.

COMMUNICATIONS CHAIRHOLDER AND COMMITTEE

DESIRED EXPERIENCE: Mid- to upper-level management in any commercial communications-service organization, including the military, utility or privately owned company.

COMMITTEE DESCRIPTION: Organizes and manages all communications-related facilities; arranges for and controls all communications needs required for smooth event operation—radios, pagers, cellular phones, etc.; works with communications utility to arrange for pay and non-pay phones where appropriate; determines and fulfills minimum phone needs in any sponsor exhibit areas; coordinates communications systems and procedures with any theme salute personnel ; coordinates all communications required to "cue" elements of performances with Entertainment Chairholder and committee; attempts to provide services at low or no cost; sets up procedures for use control and safe return of all equipment; trains all volunteers using equipment; assures that sponsor needs are met, in cooperation with Site Preparations Chairholder and committee and Sponsorship Chairholder and committee. Reports directly to Executive Director or Executive Chairholder.

SECURITY AND SAFETY CHAIRHOLDER AND COMMITTEE

DESIRED EXPERIENCE: Law enforcement official, ideally with experience in handling large venues and crowds, or private security official; work with volunteers highly desirable.

COMMITTEE DESCRIPTION: Organizes and manages all security- and safety-related facilities and areas at or immediately adjacent to site(s); works with Transportation Chairholder and committee and local agencies to provide on- and near-site motor traffic and pedestrian control, assuring ease-of-flow; cooperates with paramedic units to have qualified personnel and adequate equipment on- and near-site(s), including properly placed first-aid stations with sufficient qualified staffing, emergency vehicles, etc.; works with Transportation Chairholder and committee to assure full and immediate, unencumbered access to all areas by emergency vehicles; arranges for holding area for any misbehavables; establishes lost-child area and protective procedures; sets up and maintains lost-and-found; works with Vendor and Finance Chairholders and committees to protect any on-site cash and its transfer to banks; with all Chairholders, sets up crisis and emergency situation procedures, such as evacuation in anticipation of dangerous weather, etc.; provides and coordinates security patrols; works closely with all committees, but particularly with Site Preparations and Quality Assurance Chairholders and committees to guarantee that all areas and elements are entirely safe for all persons. Reports directly to Executive Director or Executive Chairholder.

ENTERTAINMENT CHAIRHOLDER AND COMMITTEE

DESIRED EXPERIENCE: Entertainment business management and/or bookings for musical and non-musical theatrical soloists and groups; management of arenas or theatres and their productions.

COMMITTEE DESCRIPTION: Entirely responsible for all live entertainment; assures that only the highest quality professional and volunteer/amateur entertainment and attractions are offered throughout event; creates and produces all special shows; working with Executive Director or Executive Chairholder, board and legal counsel, negotiates artist/attractions contracts at low or no cost; working with Executive Director, Executive Chairholder, Site Preparations Chairholder and committee, assures sufficient dimensions and attractive appearance of stages and all other entertainment areas; develops and maintains complete talent/attractions personnel schedule; ensures that all performers/personnel are on hand at assigned times or that suitable substitutions are on hand; issues and conducts audition calls for all talent; recruits, trains and manages individual strolling talent and participants in periodic parades; handles every aspect of on-site presence of entertainment celebrities and headliners; recruits and trains stage managers and crews; supervises arrangements for and installation of sound and lighting equipment to assure highest level of quality; sets up all PA systems and maintains control of their use; works with Site Preparations Chairholder and committee to provide adequate and secure talent dressing rooms and fully-protected equipment storage spaces; cooperates with Security and Safety Chairholder and committee to protect stage props, musical instruments, equipment, personnel, celebrities, etc., and to guard against performance-area vandalism during off hours; works with Sponsorship Chairholder and committee to assure proper sponsor credit signage and verbal recognition in entertainment areas; designs and implements ceremonies for presentation programming for all recipients of official event prizes and awards (exceptions: games with many small prizes bestowed); with Event Extension Chairholder and committee, provides entertainment taken from event lineup to perform at hospitals, indigent-care centers, senior facilities, etc. Reports directly to the Executive Director or Executive Chairholder.

GROUP ATTENDANCE CHAIRHOLDER AND COMMITTEE[8]

DESIRED EXPERIENCE: Considerable background requiring exceptional organizational skills—from first planning to final implementation; diplomatic/"effective soft-sell" salesperson; experience in group sales especially desirable.

COMMITTEE DESCRIPTION: Primary objective: TO INCREASE ATTENDANCE through organized, direct programs; organizes and implements effective programs to get groups to attend event together, particularly at predesignated times, as a means of keeping event offerings in full operation, especially during ordinarily light-attendance periods; establishes a program providing responsible adult hosts at event for unfortunate youngsters who would not be able to attend otherwise; works with Site Preparations Chairholder and committee to provide special welcome signs for each organized group; target visitor sources include but are not limited to church or synagogue and other religious organizations, retirement homes and organization, sports and athletic operations, employee associations of companies, civic and fraternal groups, youth clubs, garden societies, support groups (such as Special Olympics), law enforcement associations, labor unions, parent-teacher chapters, professional societies and guilds, military units, etc. NOTE: does not include any entertainment-related groups, who are the responsibility of the Entertainment Chairholder and committee. Reports directly to Executive Director or Executive Chairholder.

HOSPITALITY CHAIRHOLDER AND COMMITTEE

DESIRED EXPERIENCE: Mid- to upper-level management of hotels or motels; military experience in housing and mass-personnel logistics; any volunteer committee dealing with ad hoc lodging of large numbers; access to channels for inviting high governmental officials; ideally, very well versed in formal protocol and professional etiquette.

COMMITTEE DESCRIPTION: Duties are threefold:

I

Determines number, locations, designs and staffing for informational stations throughout event, both on-site and when necessary, for off-site venues and commercial locations; these multipurpose facilities should satisfy virtually every desire of all celebrants, including but not limited to needs for directions, information on performance times, schedule for any shuttle services, where to take a lost child and where to get emergency treatment; they are also centers for on-site purchase of food/beverage *script* (that part being staffed by Vendor Chairholder and committee); reporting any disturbances or problems to Security and

Safety Chairholder and committee; providing all other guest services needed to make every visit as pleasant as possible and every visitor as comfortable as possible.

II

Handles all matters related to providing housing for any participants and/or visitors; working with Entertainment Chairholder and committee, arranges suitable lodgings for entertainers; prepares procedures for accepting lodging applications, fulfilling them, and notifying requesters; sets up system for attracting and operating host-home program; responsible for handling any problems within lodgings involving event-related personnel.

III

Organizes and manages all on-site hospitality facilities; serves as official event "greeter" and protector of protocol; responsible for all on-site needs of VIP's, including entertainment and other celebrities (in cooperation with Entertainment Chairholder and committee), sponsor company officials (in conjunction with the Sponsorship Chairholder and committee), top-level media representatives (cooperating with Marketing Chairholder and committee); includes inviting and handling on-site arrangements for political VIP's — President and Vice President, governor(s), national and state legislators, mayors, city councils members, high-level law enforcement officials, firefighter executives, etc.; be resource for all Chairholders and committees to call on regarding all matters of protocol and etiquette; assures that all Chairholders and committees forward expressions of appreciation to EVERY person deserving such. Reports directly to Executive Director or Executive Chairholder.

EVENT EXTENSION CHAIRHOLDER AND COMMITTEE

DESIRED EXPERIENCE: Professional or volunteer experience with health care and/or care-giving institutions.

COMMITTEE DESCRIPTION: Primary objective: "Take event to those who can't attend it on-site;" will play major role in getting every person to attend the event who wants to; works with Entertainment Chairholder and committee to create a series of "mobile" entertainment acts from those booked for event presentation, those acts being taken to health care and/or care-giving institutions to provide pleasure and a sense of participation to those who cannot be present in person; must work closely with all hospitals, homes for the elderly and indigent, residences for encumbered individuals, etc., to see to it that all visiting acts are appropriate and programmed to fit destination needs, schedules and restrictions; also coordinates and assists churches, synagogues and other religious groups cooperating with event by relating religious services directly to it. Reports directly to Executive Director or Executive Chairholder.

SPORTS CHAIRHOLDER AND COMMITTEE

DESIRED EXPERIENCE: Professional or considerable volunteer experience with athletic programs and/or sports competitions.

COMMITTEE DESCRIPTION: Organizes and manages all sports-related facilities and activities at and near event site; arranges for and assists with management of *off-site* venues for organizing, hosting and helping with the promotion of event-affiliated sports programs, including golf, tennis, racquetball, bowling, cycling, archery, marathon, etc.; must negotiate best arrangements with each venue and establish a continuing, rewarding and positive relationship with each; makes all arrangements for *on-site* competitions, including selection and preparation of participation areas for any softball series, volleyball tournaments, soccer competitions, horseshoe contests, Frisbee® Disc championship play-offs, soapbox derbys, etc.;

works closely with Site Preparations Chairholder and committee and its decorations unit, and with Sponsorship Chairholder and committee to assure that *all* venues are well decorated with event-related decorations and with sponsor banners; works with Marketing Chairholder and committee to attract participants and to report results to all media; actively seeks recognition for event as the official host and playing site for local, regional, state and national championships of appropriate sports. Reports directly to Executive Director or Executive Chairholder.

AWARDS AND PRIZES CHAIRHOLDER AND COMMITTEE

DESIRED EXPERIENCE: Retail or wholesale sales, preferably with considerable connections and clout with merchants and potential donators of cash or in-kind prizes.

COMMITTEE DESCRIPTION: Receives from all Chairholders and committees specific needs for prizes, awards, certificates, plaques, trophies or cash for prizes; arranges for donations or minimal prices for numerous prizes; sets up security and accounting systems for prize storage and delivery to authorized recipients; assures proper recognition for donors through Sponsorship Chairholder and committee; works closely with Entertainment Chairholder and committee for presentation ceremonies; devises suitable acts and methods of expressing special appreciation to all donors from event. Reports directly to Executive Director or Executive Chairholder.

Notes

[1]Formerly known as the International Festivals Association (IFA).

[2]Salaried personnel are included in this category, but some executive volunteer administrators are nearly always needed as well, thus forming a quasi-committee.

[3]Another optional organizational plan is offered in *SE:IO*, Chapter Five. That plan is especially suitable for a brand new event, one with an anticipated actual attendance of about perhaps 50,000 to 200,000. That was the projected size of the just designed Boise River Festival, for which it was developed and which served as a case study for much of *SE:IO*. Because of a different clumping of responsibilities than those that follow herein, committee names in *SE:IO* are not always the same as those at the conclusion of this chapter. You may find that a merging or husking of these and other organizational units may be necessary in order to satisfy your specific needs. As with all event components, use that most excellent freedom of creativity liberally in your organizational planning.

[4]CD's are written compiled groups of assignments, excerpted from Position Descriptions, given to individual volunteers within that committee for implementation.

[5]Board and Executive Director or event Executive Director may elect to approach local marketing, public relations and/or advertising firms to discuss having one or more of them carry out these significant functions under in-kind sponsorship arrangements. This involvement will give it/them extraordinary access to media and other professions and business of tremendous value to it/them. Should this arrangement develop, it/they should be listed among the highest professional levels.

[6]Because of the tax-pivotal date of April 15, CPA's are generally at their professional busiest when most needed by warm-weather events; therefore, those sought in the recruitment process should be in a circumstance that permits heavy early planning involvement and minimum operational requirements until after April 30. Fill-in volunteers may be used to carry out needs until that date.

[7]See No. 4, Chapter 7, regarding recommendation that script be sold to visitors for the purchase of food and beverages, instead of using cash.

[8]Note that this title is not group SALES, since our study assumes admission-free events. Group ATTEN-DANCE is just as important here as it would be if tickets were being sold.

Chapter Seven

ENDING UP ON
THE TREADMILL

After throwing around some pretty heavy weights, as we've done in the past six chapters, let's follow the practice of many fitness fans who unwind—and give their cardiovascular systems some benefit at the same time. Machines of choice are often treadmills, which usually do the job without going anywhere. Let's hop on one, but for a change, let's make this one go somewhere.

In the remaining pages, I will present sixteen subjects that don't quite fit in any one or more sections of this book, but nevertheless are of *vital significance*. Please don't let their isolation rush you to judge them as having less importance or relevance than previous sections of this book. They definitely deserve equal attention.

Let's get on our treadmill for our final exercise.

1. LENGTH OF EVENTS

In virtually every case I have studied or been exposed to in the past several decades, I have found that virtually no community, metro area, state, regional or national event should exceed seven to ten days' duration. And many do well—*very well!*— in even less time—four, three or even two days. Obviously, all other factors being equal, I am a strong advocate of compressed, high-energy, fast-paced, sizzle-'n'-dazzle events.

Longer events simply wear out, themselves and their constituents. It is extraordinarily difficult to pull together enough *quality, truly worthwhile* offerings to keep interest level at a peak over more than ten days. Most attempts to do so end up in a roller-coaster pattern; a series of high excitement periods followed by a breath-taking drop in activity—and interest.

Long event durations generally do *very* little to encourage tourism. How many people will be willing to set aside two or more full, precious weeks out of their work year to go to an event host city offering only spotty periods of high interest offerings during that time? Not nearly as many as would do so for a condensed, high-activity event.

2. SINGLE- VS. MULTIPLE-EVENT SITES

When both options exist, and all other things being equal, I'll opt for the single site every time. Among circumstances demanding multiple sites are the need for varying, often separated sports facilities, or when there's a requirement for a mix of permanent buildings, dictated by weather, such as winter happenings. Other conditions that insist on plural venues are those very nice popularity problems: too many participants, too many cars, too many parking spaces needed, too much demand on emergency vehicles, etc. to be handled by a lone location.

But I'm bullheadedly convinced that when events *can* occupy one site (and a majority can), they absolutely *should*. Reasons:

— Obviously, it's virtually always much easier to manage one location.

— Volunteer assignments and back-ups are more efficiently handled.

— Event-goers nearly always prefer one-venue events for these reasons:

   √ They have to find only one parking space, and it can be just theirs all day.

   √ They don't have to climb in and out of summer-hot or winter-cold cars several times a day, drive to other sites, then (here it is again) look for close-by parking spaces.

   √ It's been found that the typical event-goer would be quite content to sit in one spot and be constantly entertained, with only minimal movement to get food and merchandise; one site definitely serves that profile.

— Very important: you don't have to have an off-the-meter IQ to figure out that, all other components being of high quality, sponsors *much* prefer string-of-pearls-condensed events to those with missing-bead gaps. Sponsors—sponsors who need people—get more exposure for each dollar they invest when there are crowds in a single venue, simply because they don't have to dilute bucks by having to replicate banners and other promotional exhibits over a number of sites. Remember it as "DIRES— Dollar Impact Ratio of Event Sponsorship."

   √ Decorations and other visual enhancements have a much greater impact when working together on a single site. (See Chapter 3).

   √ Duplication of necessary services (security, emergency vehicles, communications, etc.) is avoided and they're made more efficient.

   √ Entertainment performances can often play to more people in fewer presentations (possibly without repeats), each having a much greater reach.

   √ Food and merchandise sales are centralized, easing deliveries and avoiding duplication of personnel and equipment.

3. IDEAL SITE COMPONENTS

Whether you're looking for a location to place a brand new event or a better site for an existing one, you should have a check list of components to help you move in the right direction. Let me offer this series of "what-abouts":

• What about the right size? Better to have too much room than not enough. Over-estimate space needs in terms of numbers of people, of tents, of visitor cars, service vehicles . . . everything. Acre-size is mentally deceiving; it's not as big as it sounds.

- What about good site lines? A stand of redwood trees or a canyon between audience/spectators and stages tend to strain program enjoyment, to say the least.

- What about its neighborhood? Immediately adjacent stockyards, all-shift steel mills, busy airports, eight-lane superhighways, are not good.

- What about the nature and condition of the site surface? Open quick sand pits and alligator swamps are exciting but visitor-consuming. Ideal surfaces are those that will take brutal amounts of foot traffic, rain (good drainage), and temporary vehicular access paths, hold tent stakes, accommodate grass parking (if necessary) and, generally, add to the appearance of your event.

- What about hidden dangers? What's there that you can't see? Covered wells? Animal-made tunnels? Chemical leftovers? Subsurface rusty metal? Partially covered lumber with crusty nails? Have professional searches done if there's any doubt. Tetanus Fest, Broken-Ankle Relays and The Law-Suit Challenges really are not great event themes.

- What about basic necessities? Are they available? Tap capability into close-by electrical sources is nice. When they're not readily at hand, you'll likely have to use generators, which can usually be rented, a cost you should consider at the outset of budget formulation. Cable drops to bring in system electricity are ordinarily quite expensive, but check with your power company about options and cost. For most temporary sites, potable water must be brought in; contact your water company for advice and assistance.

- What about suitable traffic arteries that will satisfactorily feed the site? Are they too busy at "your times" even without event traffic? If so, look around for another site.

- What about ease of crowd flow circulation? A ten-foot-wide, two-mile long strip doesn't work real well. Reasonably proportioned, adequate-size squares, rectangles, "wide" triangles, circles or ovals generally do.

4. SCRAPS OVER SCRIPT

Here's another event subject that can cause opposing sides to give thought to open warfare: *whether to use cash or script to sell food.*

Before I reveal my choice, let's compare the characteristics of both options side-by-side. That way, if you're smart, you'll reach the same conclusion I do at the end of this section.

WHEN CASH IS USED	WHEN SCRIPT IS USED
People must stand in only one line, the one to purchase food.	People have to stand in two lines, but total linetime is reduced because no change has to be made with food purchase; script can be sold in advance of the event; and with sufficient number of script sales outlets and volunteers, script lines are often avoided or move very fast.
Food vendors much prefer it and are generally more cooperative with this practice; honor system must nearly always be used.	Script gives host event *total control* over food income. Food vendors come to accept this system over time.
Cash requires considerable security and accountability measures.	Script is usable only during the event duration, thus is less valuable than cash and does not require quite the same security and accountability intensity.
For this same reason, use of satellite food areas and those serving plural venues is more complicated and demanding.	Script *greatly* facilitates operation of satellite and multiple-site patterns. They can be set up easily and quickly, and on an as-needed basis.
Cash is easier and quicker to count.	Script can be counted after each volunteer shift and at day's end when collected from area several sources, thus reducing an enormous end-of-event ticket-counting session. Script counting machines can be rented for high-volume use.

Now, I ask you. Wasn't that an entirely fair and equitable comparison? Did you guess at any time my preference? I'm sure you did not, so let me reveal it to you now. Why, it's SCRIPT, of course!

Again, there may be mitigating circumstances that dictate use of cash, but I can't think of any, and I haven't personally witnessed any events where I thought cash would, should or could triumph over script.

A client of mine, after a year of pangs approaching childbirth intensity, converted to script after nearly ten years of cash. Those eventers were astonished at the positive reception given that conversion by food vendors, volunteers and especially the event-goers themselves. *There were very few complaints.*

Try it . . . you and your attendees just might like it.

POST-SCRIPT: Cash must be used for merchandise and any other sold service or product. If there are instances when it works, I haven't personally seen nor heard of such.

One big reason for no-script merchandise: Too wide-ranging prices. You might have a $2.95 key chain in the same case as a $20 t-shirt or a $49.95 something. For that reason, bulky script won't work.

5. BUDGETS FROM THE OUTSIDE IN

Countless variables make it impossible to suggest a budget formula that would work for every event. Or even for one perhaps. Some of you may get great entertainment at very little or no cost; others my pay big bucks for mediocre performances. Expensive transportation may face some; others may have virtually no figures under that label. And many times, prices for the very same product or service varies tremendously from one part of the country to another.

My budget advice to you is to take the sum you know you have to support your event to your accountant-finance committee head or outside consultant. Through interviews with you and your Chairholders, let that expert come up with an expense grid. Offer it to your unit heads and let them make cases, if they can, for an increase in allocations.

But whatever you do, stick to your final budget!

6. AN OPEN LETTER TO SPONSORS

Dear Sponsor:

Thank God for you!

It's long been a given that our events industry couldn't survive, certainly as we know it today, without you. And every indication is that you will play even bigger roles in the new century. It's about your future and ours that I'm writing.

If you are like most of us, you were taught in school and often by parents and other sources that you could do *anything* you want to do, if you *really* put your mind to it.

They were—and are—wrong. Dead wrong.

Many of us who have survived a whole stack of years have already recognized that fact. You may have also found, as I have, that those well-meaning back-patters and well-wishers inadvertently set us up for some pretty sizable unhappiness and frustration—and some really bad business experiences.

As well meaning as they were, they didn't take into account several major factors: our strengths (and lack there of), talents (and lack there of), interests (and lack there of) . . . or our voids, weaknesses, fears, doubts and limitations (NO lack thereof).

Each of us must acknowledge and learn to live within our own operational boundaries, which mercifully, differ from person to person. In this marvelous human gigantic jigsaw puzzle of interlocking abilities, no two "pieces" are alike. This powerful difference factor is an essential too many sponsors forget the moment they sign onto an event.

When that happens, *you the sponsor* are the one who ends up getting short-changed. In addition to any one or up to all seven[2] of the basic reasons for becoming a sponsor, you should be buying the expertise of those running the event, along with their know-how in maximizing the return on your sponsorship dollars. If you feel you must do any of their jobs for them, you aren't getting your money's worth, and you should move on to a better deal.

Because the sponsored event didn't do its job and/or due to the conviction that sponsors can and should do everything, some really poor moves that hurt sponsors have been made in lots of events. In the interest of higher quality sponsorship and more productive participation, permit me to list a few below. If you aren't guilty of any of these, great; if you are, try to avoid them in the future. Here they are, courtesy the marketers for fictitious Dynamic Dill Pickles:

— *Leave the script-writing up to those whose job is—well—script-writing.* Dynamic Dill forbade the use of any pickle jokes or poking fun at any other condiments (which that company also produced) by comedians in the comedy club show it sponsored. To be sure there was no violation, DD demanded review of scripts before each show. Comedians who couldn't produce scripts didn't perform. What was left wasn't a real funny gig. Leave show business to those who know show business.

— *Don't insist that event publicists lace their media material with too much commercialism.* Having Dynamic Dills mentioned ten times on each page of double-spaced copy is a bit much, especially if the advertising copy line is thrown in a couple of times as well. An overabundance of commercialism will almost certainly kill media material; if it does get by, you can be sure most, maybe all, commercial copy will be blue-penciled. Meanwhile, you haven't helped media relations with Dynamic Dills or the event. Accept the advice and strategy of the event marketing people.

— *Be reasonable about your sponsor banners.* If Dynamic Dills is told its bucks buy ten banners, then ten it is; the company shouldn't try to get more without upping its contribution. If banners are specified to measure two-by-ten feet, the company shouldn't try to get enlargements. And DD shouldn't insist that banners get any better play than it was guaranteed at contract signing. That especially includes trying to upstage (literally) banners of higher-level, bigger paying sponsors. Leave banner strategy to the event's sponsorship group.

— *Be reasonable about sponsor perks.* Dynamic Dills was told it would get ten tickets to reserved seats at several shows, ten passes to the Sponsor Hospitality Tent, and five reserved-parking stickers. Now, leave it there. Its president shouldn't turn up at the Hospitality Tent with a party of   twenty because "oh, they won't care; they can always make room for a few more." It's not fair for DD to demand more than it paid for while other sponsors stick to their original deals, especially those that paid more money.

— *Don't name a sponsored facility by incorporating all the sell messages and descriptions on a product label or from its ad campaign.* People laugh at you when they hear the emcee say, "Welcome, ladies and gentlemen, to the Dynamic Uncooked Baby Dill Pickle that Goes Great with Hamburgers If You Serve Them Cold (the Pickles, that is) Stage." (Okay, a bit of a hyperbole, but not much.) Your image has NOT been enhanced. "Dynamic Dill Pickle Stage" is so much more acceptable—and image *is* enhanced.

— *In summary, behave as if you have bought a sponsorship, not a crown.*

When an event is on your side because you're so pleasant to deal with, you will accrue a surprising number of extras not included in any written bargain. Virtually every time, really nice sponsors get back-bending cooperation; nasty ones get front-bending views of backsides, subtle or hidden though they may be. It's a sure thing, for example, that if media show up and need guidance, letting the event publicist select "best-to-see," you can bet that event media folks will see to it that Nice, Inc., will definitely get visited.

On to another important matter. Those of you (and there are many) who plop down the sponsorship check and walk away dusting your hands are decimating your sponsorship impact. You should have a plan developed already (or pretty quickly after sponsorship purchase) to maximize marketing of your involvement.

It is not at all unusual for smart sponsors to spend $8 to $10—even more—per dollar of sponsorship on "marketing" their investment. Plans include advertising and publicity in powerful trade publications or general-public media, whichever reaches their best targets. Business-to-business dealings can also be greatly enhanced by a sponsor taking high-value customers to that event, and giving them treatment befitting royalty or a Mafia don.

In closing, let me say again how much the events industry owes you . . . and how much more productive your sponsorship dollars can be with the right investment and in supporting that investment.

Our plea: just let us help you more.

AN ADDED NOTE FOR EVENTERS RELATIVE TO SPONSORS:

Don't apologize to event-goers for giving sponsors reserved seating in preferential areas and other perks at free or very low-admission events. In fact, in a friendly manner, your emcee for a presentation where there is such a benefit should take the initiative and call the audience's/spectator's attention to the presence of sponsors "down here in the front row" whose generosity has made this free presentation possible "for all of you." He/she should call for a round of applause for sponsors.

---

7. LOATHSOME *LOP*SIDEDNESS

Until recent years, it was a joy for me to work with so many business and commercial operations which were so frequently sparkling examples of efficiency, productivity, organizational strength and *time-awareness*. However, too often recently, I have found cases where a creeping menace is no longer creeping:

Lack *Of P*lanning, what I call *LOPsidedness.*

Perhaps it's a reliance on modern technology that has lulled many into believing that computer can speedily take care of any planning needs, doing it so quickly that people can wait until the last minute to make crucial moves.

HEY, FOLKS, *IT'S NOT WORKING!*

All too frequently in my day-to-day work I'm called on Monday to be asked to have an event in place Thursday—an event that should be given at least two to three weeks of prep time, just to make it work adequately, never mind with true quality.

Unfortunately, LOPsidedness is chewing its way more everyday into the special event organism. One example: sponsors tell me that one of their biggest continuing—and constantly growing—complaints is having sponsorship opportunities offered with too little implementation and promotion time. That's LOPsidedness in its rawest form.

Regardless of technological advances in the 21ˢᵗ Century, *nothing* will ever replace the human-instituted need to plan ahead. It provides time for development of quality, reduces the acid of unnecessary stress, makes work a pleasure and definitely increases the ratio of dollars to results.

What can you as eventers do about LOPsidedness? Some suggestions:

— Don't be guilty of it yourself. **Plan on plenty of planning** . . . in *every*thing. Err on the side of what you think will be more planning time than you might need.

— **Provide companies with which you do business a timeline** that allows for any LOPsidedness on their part. But hide it well, by adding hours and days where they "won't show." If looseness in your timeline is discovered, all your extra hours and days will be company-devoured—and you'll find yourself on a crushing schedule after all.

— **If you can't pad your time estimate, be up front with your client;** explain that you can get the job done in the allowed for too-little time, but if a good serving of quality is a goal, you simply must have more time. Granted, there are conditions that will exist that will give you no choice; you'll have to move ahead without minimal time to do your job as well as you could have otherwise. All you can do is give it your best and hope for . . . well—the best!

8. WIN OR LOSE WITH BOOZE?

Big question: should we allow alcoholic beverages at our event? Am I indecisive on this big question? Well, yes and no. Let's discuss the subject, then you decide.

BOTTOMS UP   Opens lucrative opportunities for beverage sponsorships. Brewers are among the most frequent and generous sponsors.

THUMBS DOWN   Especially at family-oriented events. Many prefer to enjoy themselves in an alcohol-free atmosphere, especially where there are large numbers of youngsters.

BOTTOMS UP   You *can* have it both ways: alcohol can be served in a restricted area ("The Beer and Wine Garden"); drink must stay within those boundaries.

THUMBS DOWN   But drinkers often dislike being separated from their families or parties, not being able to dine with them while they're consuming strong beverages unless they (and their children) come into the beer/wine reserve.

BOTTOMS UP   What's a late-night event for young adults without suds and spirits?

THUMBS DOWN   Security people and law enforcers virtually always vote for no on alcohol at these events, especially if they are late-night, young-adult segments. They support their views by pointing to driving dangers, various forms of harassment, brawling, out-of-control horse-play, etc.

BOTTOMS UP   "We're adults and we should be permitted to act like adults, including having a responsible amount of alcohol while we're having a good time with family and friends."

THUMBS DOWN   There's too much of a temptation for adults to buy and furnish alcohol to under-agers. It's too easy to do at a special event.

MY RECOMMENDATION:

I believe the drinking policy, along with all other event aspects, should reflect the nature or choice of the community. Events in or near New York City, Chicago, San Francisco or Los Angeles require different programming and atmosphere than those in or near Salt Lake City and other communities where prevailing religious beliefs or practices or local customs preclude booze and other programmables found elsewhere.

It really depends on the event classification. I can see beer and wine at sports competitions before I can at all-city, family-oriented festivals.

9. IT'S YOUR CALL

This matter, which seems rather petty (but it really isn't) applies to civilization as a whole, but I'm hoping that our industry will lead others out of the dark ages of—

BAD PHONE MANNERS AND MATTERS

FACT: the telephone is our **most used** communications device. **FACT:** the telephone is also our **most abused** communications device.

Why we must be reminded of the following is an unsolved mystery, but we do, so take at look.

- ### PLEASE RETURN *ALL* PHONE CALLS.

It's not baseball. America's favorite pastime is *ignoring* phone calls. And there are big bunches of people playing this obnoxious game. If you possibly can, at least make a quick call to say your schedule won't permit an adequate conversation just now but you'll call later. And do it. If you can't make even that quick call, ask someone else to make it for you. Or short—*short!*— vocal messages on machines might take care of that need.

- ### HANDLE WITH CARE: VOCAL MESSAGING.

Will you *please* not record an outgoing greeting message of longer duration than a Wagner opera. Check out this only slightly exaggerated Imaphone Irritant's message:

"Hi! Sorry I can't take your call just now. I'm either on another line or in the bosses' office getting chewed for being late this morning, or I'm getting my first cup of coffee, or I might have stepped out a moment to get dry cleaning I dropped off two weeks ago, or goodness knows what else! I should be back around three o'clock, unless a possible staff meeting is called, in which case I'll have get back to you tomorrow. Oh, my! Tomorrow's Saturday. Well, make it after I get back from my vacation, which starts Monday. I'm going to . . . chatter, chatter, chatter."

Without being cute or curt, in a pleasant voice, simply invite the caller to leave a *brief* message. Chances are excellent that the caller is smart enough to know that you didn't personally answer the phone and doesn't require a litany of reasons why you didn't.

If you are about to enter a situation paralleling a cloistered religious order, suggest that the caller contact another person, giving name and number—with that person's prior permission, of course. That just might curtail an infinite number of phone tries, each of which is more infuriating than the last to the serial caller.

Further, please don't purchase one of those answering devices that lengthens the beep with the accumulation of calls. There's nothing more cloying than an interminable, uninterrupted B-flat whine while you're waiting to leave history's most important message and you *really* must go to the bathroom.

And please don't leave messages that detail your life from conception to that moment. Brevity, brevity, brevity!

Do try to be more humanly charming than the mechanical telephone lady, who says, "If you'd like to make a call, please hang up and try again . . ."

On those rare occasions when you connect directly with a living, breathing human on the phone, remember that the overall texture of each phone conversation is nearly always firmly patterned in the first two or three seconds. If you're having a bad-hair day, try to get someone else to handle telephoning. Rent some movies on your way home.

10. DETAILS, DETAILS, DETAILS

By the time you've reached this point in my book, you should have determined for yourself that special events require detailed handling of details. If you do not work well with details—if you do not have truly a ravenous appetite for dealing with countless but important fine points—then I suggest you seek a much less detail-oriented pursuit such as neurosurgery,child-raising, theoretical physics, or (heaven help you!) celestial mechanics.

Deft detailing can be a natural talent or an acquired trait (with a bit of dedicated effort). It pivots on the development of an ability to recognize and prioritize every factor—every item—in a given entity. It's knowing how and when to deal with one detail while using mental White-Out® on another.

Here are some nearly unbelievable instances (call them pet peeves or whatever, they're still meaningless details) that I have encountered over the years:

— A band director who suffered melt-down when a member's shoes were not laced left-over-right

— That poster boy for the Temper-Tantrum Troupe who just lost it when anyone called and asked, "is SHE in" (his name is Chris)

— An executive director who insisted that *all* documents—checks, reports, plans, etc.—be signed only— ONLY—in black ink (they were sent back if blue, green or red were used)

— A CEO of a high-paying sponsor company who demanded a daily count by phone of the number of sheets of paper used in his company's photocopier on duty at an event ("excessive" use had to be personally justified)

— A sponsor who issued a kind of demerit to anyone in his company using the information operator in any city for any reason (despite the fact that such a practice often requires less time—and therefore, less money—than retrieving a phone book or logging onto the Internet, searching for the listing amid highly misleading or confusing headings . . . and finally placing the call)

11. UNWANTED: SPECIAL EVENTS

Crack houses, tire-burning facilities, pre-teen sweatshops and any kind of special event that attracts a goodly number of visits. Some people hate them all. Equally.

Since most of us are so much in love with our work, we find it difficult to believe that there are those who become sun-braving vampires at the mere thought of new or enlarged special events near their own private caskets. They say they're okay for anyplace else, but not for their domain. It's called NIMBY – "not in my backyard."

Who are these poor misguided souls? Law enforcement officials often lead the pack, followed closely by those in traffic, park and city maintenance departments, trash collectors, ecologists, and commercial interests who fear profit-gulping by the temporary intruder. Another big opposition lobby: people in existing, nearby smaller events who betray their lack of confidence in their own happenings by fearing whale gobbling of their minnows.

A few years ago, I designed a very carefully thought-out special event for a consortium of contiguous cities, but my plans didn't get very far. They were summarily dispatched with a hit on delete keys by an amalgam of law enforcers and community-eventers. Stated reasons: traffic snags, crime, drunks, rowdy people (especially kids), blocked driveways, entertainment blast-noise, trampled lawns, and so on. And my plans were just too big, they claimed.

Despite a near certain promise of $20 million to $30 million in eventual incremental income for those communities—not to mention big bucks in overtime to be paid to professional law enforcers for event security—all declared my plans "unwanted" and the event fetus was aborted, community eventers assisting in the operation.

They gave no quarter to my carefully-crafted measures to overcome *every one* of those fears. I had even developed a concept where the new festival would serve as a regional (eventually a national) device for promoting attendance (for a while) at the smaller events, held before, during and after the proposed new mega-festival.

It was my hope that, eventually, the new festival would be magnetic to those smaller ones, enfolding them—*with the avid consent of their leaders and communities*—as major units of an event having true quality and national stature. See No. 12 below.

Nevertheless, eyes and ears closed. Real best interests in the betterment of the community were over-ridden. I lost—and so did the people of that area. As did their would-be tourists.

What can be done to counter such actions? If a potential host community has powerful elected or civic leaders eager for added income and prestige from an event, they might be able to override any opposition. Get to them early, the moment you have well-thought-out plans and list of solid-gold, indisputable advantages of the proposed event for the community. They just might join the fight on your side.

News media are often strong influences in such campaigns. Their editorial weight can be very formidable, wielded by the stories they choose to carry, the manner in which those stories are put together, the selection of people for sound bites or quotes and their overt opinion statements. If you can establish credibility with them and lay out your proof of the advantages as best you can, you have a pretty good chance of magnetizing these groups as allies. Media generally tend to favor events, but don't take their support for granted. Ever!

(Neither of these options were available to me in the aforementioned case.)

Such resistance will almost certainly become more pervasive as we enter the new century. There will be larger populations, causing events to proliferate and become larger. Greater numbers and sizes of events will stoke just that many more hot coals of hostility toward them. Which brings me to my next point.

12. THERE ARE TOO MANY EVENTS RIGHT NOW

"How can an event advocate advocate fewer events?," you ask. Because my credo is "more quality than quantity." And I've repeatedly found good reasons for reaching that conclusion. If we're to have better events, we must permit only the survival of the fittest.

Surprisingly large numbers of metro areas have many hundred *regular* events annually. In warm months, far too many share several of the same days. Some span identical time frames.

Here are the problems caused by the overflow of the event numbers cup:

— **There are just so many good volunteers,** each having only so many hours to donate. If you were to skim off the cream of the volunteer mix from scores of less-effective events and put them to work on fewer-but-better (not necessarily bigger) ones, just think of the quality improvement those events would enjoy! And how much happier our publics would be, not to mention the volunteers themselves and certainly event sponsors.

— Regarding sponsors: **There are just so many sponsorship dollars available.** Each year, sponsors are becoming increasingly savvy; they are demanding more and more impact for every invested dollar. Century 21 sponsors, more so than in their 20th Century programs, are going to go for the kind of quality that attracts the quantity of opportunities satisfying one or more of their marketing objectives. Events that don't improve through check-ups will inevitably become check-outs.

— **Better events will bring out better crowds.** Despite the proliferation of events in the past three or four decades, there are still millions of people who are stay-aways and many companies who are not buying sponsorship strategy. Why? Certainly lack of quality is one reason – the inability of many events to satisfy corporate needs.

> **NOTE:** In my speeches on this subject, I have sometimes been strongly attacked for being "anti-small events." **CATEGORICALLY UNTRUE.** I have enjoyed several very fit, pony-size thoroughbreds that would induce high pride in any community. Conversely, I have seen some big-time, morbidly obese beasts that are hard put to justify their existence.

13. MERGERS

Quality can very frequently result from deftly combining events, particularly those that are entirely volunteer-driven. Here's why:

— Duplication, even triplication, of volunteer jobs can be eliminated.

— In other instances, this move strongly encourages volunteer shift grids (see Chapter 6).

— One heavy-up marketing effort can be almost always more effective than two or more lesser ones.

— Buying power is bolstered because of higher volume purchasing.

— Combined budgets can buy better entertainment.

— It's a virtually certainty: all event-goers prefer a big-name event with big-name talent, big-name sponsors, big-name VIP's *and big-time organizational know-how.*

— Sponsor dollars invariably increase and each dollar buys more when there is one higher quality event available to them.

Interestingly in event merging, opposites can sometimes attract each other as much as matchables. Example:

> Suppose in your community there is "The Capital City Arts & Crafts Festival," a fairly fair event, held every August. There is also "The Capital City Sportstacular," equally okay, held in June. Finally, there is "The Capital City Contemporary Music Fest," traditionally a Memorial Day weekend event. All three are entirely volunteer-staffed.

> Now, let's symbolically combine them under the name, "The Capital City Free-For-All Festival," to be held henceforth annually during the five most appropriate days nearest summer's Day One (about June 21), since, at present, event numbers are somewhat smaller than in the event-cluttered months of July and August. Each former separate entity decides to keep only its best components (and maybe add a few). And in the particular case, multiple sites, for sports, are necessary. As a unified operation, here's what happens:

√ A single large budget, amplified by the natural sponsor money-pull of a bigger festival, permits the hiring of a good administrator, most likely an executive director, unthinkable for the three former stand-alones. Perhaps even another staff member or two, full or part-time, can also be considered.

√ Executive volunteer posts for each of the three units remain in existence, each being a specialist in that endeavor and serving as an assistant to the new executive director or other paid staffer.

√ This person must, of course, be entirely impartial in dealings with the three divisions.[1]

√ Merging opposites still makes volunteer shifts an appealing, really powerful new option (Chapter 6).

√ Food and merchandise vendors have to organize only once instead of three times yearly; yet, a more likely larger number of people will be on hand to buy their goods.

√ Creative, generic decorations can go a long way toward gluing together the three different subjects—and through power volume purchasing, decorations can proliferate.

√ Careful planning will prove that common supplies needed for the new, enlarged event can be purchased for considerably less than the aggregate spent by the former three independents.

√ A confederation of marketing people from the former single events can each handle his/her own specialty (arts, music, sports), yet combine talents to market the festival effectively as a whole.

√ Sponsors love the new amalgamation. There are more people attracted to a single, well-presented event than the combined number visiting the three smaller, less impactful ones. Remember: sponsors need people.

√ Tourists find *much* more impetus for arranging their holidays to pivot on a festival satisfying so many interests. Everybody in the family, and adult singles as well, can find something of interest to them. That goes for the hometown folks, too.

√ And both groups find it more appealing because, for example, the sports-oriented might explore possibly new arts interests ("as long as we're here, why not?") and vice-versa.

√ It's virtually assured: the whole is definitely greater than its combined former parts in terms of the economic impact on the host community. *And in its overall quality!*

14. CAN AN EVENT BECOME TOO LARGE?

Absolutely. Even though that's a nice problem to have, it's still a problem.

When an event reaches its own level of saturation, self-trimming tends to kick in. When event-goers begin to enjoy it less because there are too many people, when the venues become too large or widely separated, when parking is really difficult and shuttling takes up too much time and/or is too clumsy, when there are too many program choices to make, constituents will start staying away.

Some events bordering on that condition actively de-promote themselves. They curtail or institute only reactive (replacing pro-active) marketing, frequently designed to level out periods-of-attendance peaks and valleys. During the event run, many ask for radio time to advise people to avoid their site(s).

Can you prevent an event from crossing over into the too-large category? Most likely not, since the line marking the boundaries of that condition is pretty elusive, fairly well smeared. Most often, you may not know you're too large until you are. If you're astute enough to see it, then you'll institute the measures described above, just as if you'd already crossed into the too-large classification.

15. RAIN TIMES TWO

Rain dates: should they be scheduled? Most events do not offer bad-weather rescheduling, simply because it's generally too expensive. An entertainment act very often will require "a rain deposit," since their booking time has been reserved twice. And what happens if it rains on the rain date?

Weather is the most impactful and uncontrollable aspect of event planning and production. Determine best play dates by an advance visit with your local U.S. Weather Bureau, asking for meteorological profiles over candidate periods of time for the last twenty-five years, then make your selection.

But don't for a moment think you're home safe by selecting the most historically weather-friendly play span. One southern event staff selected its dates after depth studies of weather patterns, only to be rained on nine consecutive years!

Almost invariably, rain-date plays don't draw the crowds that first-scheduled events will, simply because original timing has usually been well publicized and people have made arrangements to attend. Encore timing doesn't have those advantages.

Unless you can get a performer deal you can afford and you feel you can blast out an invitation to the replay dates, sufficient to get good attendance, pray for good weather the first time around.

16. EVENT PACING

Your goal as the world's most successful eventer is or will be to leave your audiences and spectators absolutely exhausted, gasping for breath, totally worn out, almost dangerously fatigued — and still begging for more.

Media are always counting ahead of citywide power outages, major blizzards and storms, etc., to see how much of an impact they have had on birth increase statistics. Your really busy event should have exactly the opposite result.

Most of us tire easily and quickly of exclamation points, but here are some suggestions for all but doing in your event-goers that absolutely warrant (!):

— Make it sizzle with speed, action and variety!

— Don't let up; it should be a rush a second!

— Have it be a seemingly seamless fabric of superimposed activity patterns

— Make your event m-o-v-e and *look like* it's moving (see Decorations)!

— During the day, no music should be slower than a perky march tempo!

— Evening dances may include slower music, but maintain a ratio favoring rapid-fire tempi! (Okay, tempOS)

— Bring in some new offerings each day (which also substantially increases repeat visits)!

— Don't let stages be empty longer than it takes to make a *fast* set-up change!

— Offer an impossible menu of a things-to-do program grid!

— Schedule frequent street-performer, costumed character and/or other interesting parades!

— March a band throughout each venue between and during parades!

— Fly something overhead at all times—kites, model planes, fireworks, streamers, environmentally-friendly balloons—anything!

— Display maximum amounts of merchandise!

— Offer an overflowing cornucopia of fabulous food and drink!

— Entice them with prize-based games—all the time!

— BIG ENERGETIC OPENING PROGRAM!

— AND, BY ALL MEANS, A BIG ENERGETIC CLOSING SPECTACULAR!

> . . . AND THERE IT WAS, AT LAST! YOU HAVE JUST WITNESSED MY OWN CLOSING. HOW WAS IT? YOU TELL ME THE NEXT TIME WE MEET. *AT YOUR VERY, VERY SPECIAL EVENT!*

Notes

[1] From Chapter One, *SE:IO*— enhance image to shape customer attitudes; drive sales; create positive publicity to heighten visibility; differentiate sponsor's product from competitors'; play good corporate citizen role; contribute to community economic development; and enhance business, consumer and VIP relations.

[2] Events with paid positions already filled are much less likely to benefit from large-event mergings since they would have to be pretty close to industrial size already in order to afford paid staff. Merging could produce a Frankenstein monster. Bringing together, say, two small, all-volunteer events under the aegis of a larger, paid-staff version might work, but be prepared to increase paid-staff salaries accordingly.

ABOUT THE AUTHOR

ROBERT JACKSON has actually had concurrent careers in special events and publicity. He began both when on the staff of the Walt Disney organization, starting at WED Enterprises, Inc., then a company personally owned by Walt Disney. WED and its subsequent repositioning as a Walt Disney company, planned, designed, and supervised construction of all Disney theme parks and their later-added attractions.

Following Disney's death, Jackson relocated to Disneyland where, as Publicity Manager, he was involved in the planning and implementation of the California theme park's many special events.

He then joined the federal government as Director of Media Services for the (now titled) United States Travel and Tourism Administration in the Department of Commerce. His role called for considerable involvement with special events and their producers throughout the nation, events being a primary instrument for attracting foreign tourists and encouraging within-nation travel by U.S. residents.

Still with the government, Jackson moved into the position of Director of Public Relations and Advertising for the John F. Kennedy Center for the Performing Arts in Washington, D.C. Again, his duties included pivotal participation in the Center's extensive special events programming.

Later, at General Mills, Inc., he was Manager of Product Publicity and Event Marketing for the company's more than 200 brand units. Jackson planned a number of events for General Mills and created its system for processing an average of more than 4,000 sponsorship proposal annually.

In recent years, Jackson has served national companies and agencies as an independent special events and publicity consultant. He suspended agency operations to accept the two-year post of Special Events Manager for the 1991 International Special Olympics Games played in Minneapolis/ St. Paul, Minnesota. Since 1992, he has been affiliated with INNOVA Marketing, Minneapolis, Minnesota.